THE
LONDON
&
BIRMINGHAM
A RAILWAY OF CONSEQUENCE

David Jenkinson

Capital Transport

First published 1988

ISBN 185414 102 3

Published by Capital Transport Publishing
38 Long Elmes, Harrow Weald, Middlesex

Printed by The KPC Group, Ashford, Kent

© David Jenkinson 1988

Front Cover
The first eighty or so miles of the London and Birmingham Railway was always and still is the spinal cord of the main line services out of Euston and this classic view of Camden bank shows the line in this mode – Stanier 'Coronation' Class 8P 4-6-2 No.46240 *City of Coventry* making easy work of the 1:70 ascent with the northbound 'Caledonian'. The picture cannot be dated with certainty but was taken between 1958 (when the engine became red with BR style lining as shown) and 1962 when it was given the LMS style of lining, more appropriate to the livery. (Ransome-Wallis Collection, courtesy NRM)

Back Cover
These two views of Camden Loco in 1958 epitomise the final days of steam on the old L&BR. The upper view shows the shed itself (on the left) with the abandoned 1847 Roundhouse in the right distance, itself a replacement for the original depot – see inside front cover. The identifiable locomotives are Class 3F 0-6-0 T No.47529 and Class 5 4-6-0 No.45339. In the second picture, Stanier 'Princess' Class 8P 4-6-2 No.46207 *Princess Arthur of Connaught* passes the depot and gets into its stride with a down Liverpool express as it begins to swing left for Primrose Hill Tunnel. (R.C. Riley)

A 1938 scene at Birmingham New Street

CONTENTS

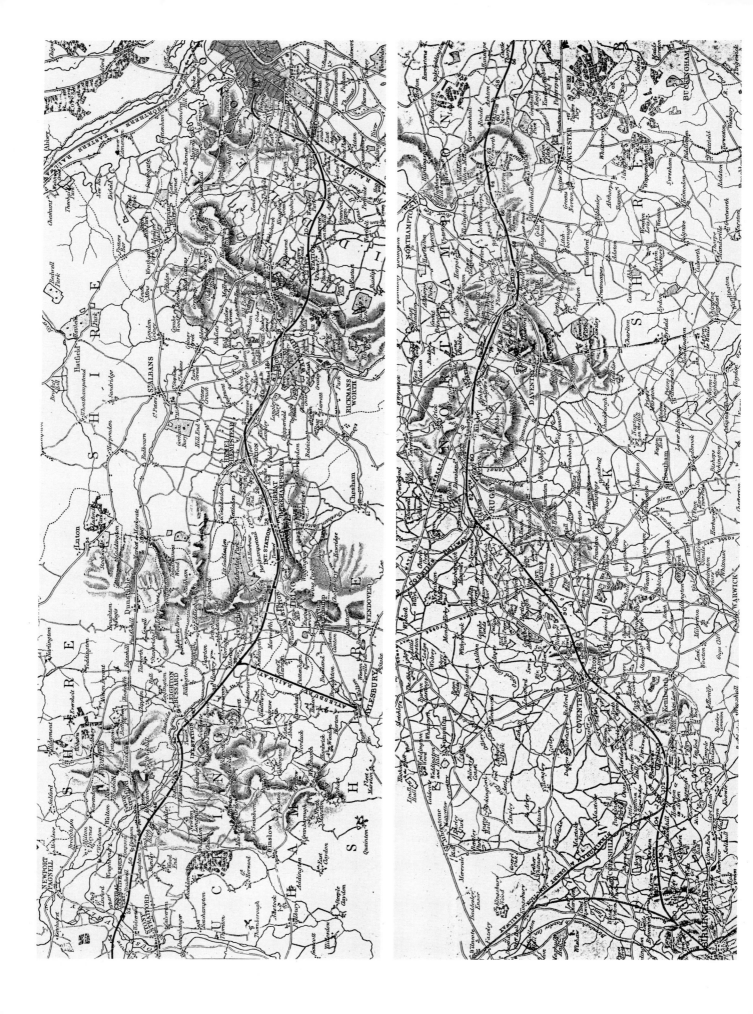

INTRODUCTION

There is a recent (peculiarly British?) custom of celebrating 150th anniversaries, particularly on the railways and possibly even influenced by them. There have been a fair number since those for the Stockton and Darlington Railway back in 1975 – and doubtless there will be more – but of all of them, that pertaining to London's first real trunk railway would probably merit pride of place, if only because there can only be one 'first' example of anything so profoundly significant. It not only showed the way in engineering terms and by establishing concepts and ideas which the whole world followed, but, by making the sort of mistakes which are the lot of any pioneer, it also showed subsequent copyists what not to do as well. Above all, it worked, survived and is still the principal long distance railway artery out of London – and its effect was to be seen in far more ways than would have been apparent at the time of its building.

Thoughts like this prompted this book. It is not a detailed academic history; there is much of that in print already. Nor is it an attempt to catalogue every single fact or artefact, static or mobile, of the London and Birmingham Railway and its successors; most of that too is in print somewhere. I hope, however, that it might be seen as more than just a celebration of a noteworthy anniversary, important though this undoubtedly is. In these pages, in a series of essays on what I consider to be some of the more interesting aspects of its history, I have tried to 'place' this railway both in space and time as a prime ingredient in the development of modern Britain – to give it some sort of historical perspective if you like – and in pursuit of this objective, I have tried to bring the story right up to the present day.

In attempting to understand this story, it is necessary to remember that the London and Birmingham Railway never stood in isolation. It was always part of a larger network which ultimately linked London with the far north of Scotland. It will thus be necessary, from time to time, to extend the discussion into this wider arena, if only to clarify the extent to which it helped set the shape of Britain during the railway age.

The 'Railway Age' proper began with the first fully mechanised form of land transport (the Liverpool and Manchester Railway of 1830), rapidly killed off most of the effective competition from either stage coach or canal and then lost its near monopoly with the development of mechanised road transport. One might, perhaps, stretch the end-point as far as 1914, but by then the true railway age was over; thereafter the ribbons of steel had to fight their corner with the increasingly sophisticated alternatives both by land and in the air. Moreover, and this makes an interesting psychological point(!), these new competitors were perceived by some to be more 'modern' and therefore 'better' than the old established railway, thereby attracting to themselves a host of supporters who simply wanted to be in fashion. But no-one can take away from the mechanised railway its role as the pioneer of *all* modern transport, setting the pattern of much that was simply copied by the later alternative forms. Therefore, since the L&BR played such a seminal role in setting this total railway pattern, it seemed worthwhile to take a deliberate look at it from this standpoint.

Written history perhaps says as much about the age in which it is written as it does about the events it records and there is little doubt that for much of the last generation, many historians have echoed the national self-doubt of a country ridding itself of empire and seeking a new role. If this indeed be a true assessment, then it would be vain to expect our institutions to be excluded. But if it is also true that Britain is growing in self-confidence and esteem in the late 1980s, then can the railways share this too, I wonder?

In essence, what I have tried to do in this account is to offer a reminder of what I happen to believe is a rattling good story of human endeavour, with lots of powerful visual imagery in support; it is a tale moreover, which I hope does not want for factual accuracy on my part in its re-telling, regardless of the freely-admitted subjectivity of some of my personal views. If, however, in its unfolding, it also manages to hold up some sort of mirror to 150 years of British history, its hopes and its fears, its triumphs and its failures, its confident beginnings followed by its self-doubt and, hopefully, renaissance, then I shall be even better pleased.

Knaresborough, July 1988   DAVID JENKINSON

Chapter 1

A NEW SORT OF TRANSPORT LINK

Viewed from a perspective of 150 years, it is hard to conceive the impact that the first trunk railways made upon this country, either physically or socially; yet they represent one of the major turning points in history.

The first of them all was the line out of London to the Midlands city of Birmingham and on to Lancashire. At the time, although its promoters no doubt had many grand visions and ideals, it is doubtful if even they could have realised what a profound effect their efforts ultimately would have, stretching far into the future and starting a story, still incomplete today. The real story, however, began some considerable time before the first train pulled out of Euston Station for Birmingham, and to put the whole business into perspective, we first need to back off into the early 18th Century, wherein lay its fundamental origins.

During that century Britain experienced the start of what historians and economists now call the 'Industrial Revolution'. In 1712, a relatively unknown Devonian, Thomas Newcomen, built the world's first practical steam engine. It was, in fact, a steam pump but, taken in conjunction with the first instance of cheap iron smelted by coke rather than charcoal in 1709 (by Abraham Darby at Coalbrookdale), one has the two primary ingredients of industry: cheap and accessible basic raw material from which to make machinery and potentially unlimited power to drive such machines.

The sheer success of 18th Century industry, supplemented as it was from an early stage by even more sophisticated machinery (much of which was eventually driven by stationary 'rotative' steam engines developed originally by James Watt), quickly drew attention to a third primary ingredient for success, the availability of good transport. The unit of prime movement was the horse, and transport was largely geared to what this animal could handle; it was not enough in many cases.

In spite of improving roads (largely by the expedient of turnpiking existing routeways), the building of canals and the establishment of horse-drawn railways of various kinds (usually to bring minerals from quarry or mine to a nearby waterway), the basic fact remained that sooner or later any 'horse-dominated' transport system was bound to run into difficulties both in terms of load size and transit speed. Machines which could increase the output of a single employee by ten times (a not untypical figure in the textile industry) could only function effectively if the transport system could handle this increase, for both incoming raw material and outgoing finished product. It frequently could

not, so, to some extent, industry was in danger of stifling itself by its own success and, in consequence, did not always expand as quickly as might have been possible.

Clearly, the need was to find some way to mechanise the transport side of the equation but it is doubtful if contemporary society saw it as such. If it did, then the subsequent growth of awareness was painfully slow.

It took nearly a century after Newcomen until, in 1804, a Cornishman, Richard Trevithick, put to work the world's first successful steam 'locomotive engine' at Pen-y-darren in South Wales – and then largely to win a wager! However, for a generation or so, these newfangled machines (Trevithick had numerous imitators and copyists) were seen as no more than a convenient horse substitute in the mining and mineral industries. There was also, it is true, more than a little experimentation about these early locomotives which made them suspect. They were high pressure machines (intrinsically and potentially more dangerous than the comfortably lower pressure stationary examples), they were not always too well made and they were anything but universally reliable – technology still had some way to go. But above all, with hindsight, the overall lack of perception as to their potential seems the most

The Stephensons, father and son.

6

surprising factor, given the ever growing problems of industrial transport. In the event, it was to be a humble and one-time illiterate Northumbrian who turned out to have the right combination of both skill and vision to make the breakthrough. His name, of course, was George Stephenson.

Stephenson did not invent the railway, the steam locomotive, nor many other things often attributed to him — though he actually *did* invent a miner's safety lamp coincidentally with Sir Humphry Davey — but he did have the breadth of intellect which allowed him to see the potential of the steam railway far more clearly than most of his contemporaries. By all accounts, he could, at times, be a bit of a prickly customer and did not always endear himself to others nor plead his cause as well as he might; but it was not for nothing that he was eventually to become known as the 'Father of the Railways' and but for him, the L&BR and its many imitators might never have taken form the way they did.

The true seed corn of modern transport was planted between Liverpool and Manchester in 1830 when the world's first fully mechanised Inter-City railway (it was not really long enough to rate as a true trunk line) was opened for both passenger and freight. The line was built by George Stephenson himself and was initially powered by locomotives of the 'Rocket' type (including 'Rocket' itself, winner of the famous Rainhill trials of 1829) which had been developed by George's son Robert, along with Henry Booth, at the family firm in Newcastle-upon-Tyne. These two ingredients — the line itself and the nature of its prime-movers — established the essential elements of what might best be called the 'Stephensonian' concept of railways and the London and Birmingham was the first trunk line out of any nation's capital city to be built on these principles. However, before going onto the specifics of the L&BR, a few further words in explanation are necessary.

George and Robert Stephenson, for they should now be considered together, were, more than any other pioneers, responsible for the establishment of central fundamental principles which stood the test of time. Firstly, they realised the desirability of good civil engineering. The steam locomotive could climb gradients and negotiate curves, but the nearer 'straight and level' the alignment of the railway could be made, the easier it was to move traffic efficiently. Both were fine civil engineers as the L&BR was itself to bear witness in the case of one of them.

Secondly, it was early during the Stephenson period that the mechanised railway developed its all-embracing yet exclusive status. In the early days, railways were conceived, rather like roads and canals, as being traffic arteries which anyone could use provided they had a suitable conveyance. The need for disciplined traffic regulation (to avoid accidents on a fixed line of rails) quickly gave rise to the realisation that consistency of standards was paramount and that this could best be achieved by the railway itself owning the locomotives and rolling stock as well as the right of way. The Liverpool and Manchester quickly demonstrated the soundness of this idea and became, henceforth, the standard pattern for the bulk of subsequent railway development.

A third element, already touched on, was their capacity to 'think big' in terms of future needs. The L&MR was quite a short route, albeit bigger than anything which had gone previously but the Stephensons — and here, perhaps, one should give George the major share of the credit — were amongst the earliest pioneers to conceive the possibility of a national network. The route north from Euston was the first tangible outcome of such thinking.

Finally, both these great men appreciated that quality and precision were crucial to mechanised transport. Early steam locomotives had often been cobbled together with techniques mostly approximating those of the village blacksmith; indeed for all we know of some of them, this may well have been the literal truth. George Stephenson realised at an early stage that precision in manufacture was a key to reliability and his son took this to an even more developed form. It is no surprise, therefore, that the modern concept of mechanical engineering

Bourne lithograph of the Regent's Canal bridge, 1838. The view is looking west with Euston to the left, Camden Town to the right.

Bury bar-framed 2–2–0 locomotive No.28, built in 1838 for the opening of the L&BR typifies a characteristic alternative early form of development after the early Stephenson ideas. The basic configuration was much the same but the framing differed – see also Chapter 4.

Facing Page The Stephenson approach to locomotive design stood the test of time. In this posed 1930 view, a replica of the Liverpool and Manchester *Rocket* stands alongside a typical 'Crewe' type of the 1840s (the preserved *Columbine* in fact) and one of the then latest express types, 'Royal Scot' 4–6–0 No.6135 *Samson*. The basic configuration of all three was much the same in all essentials.

also finds its origins in the work of the Stephensons. George was the founder and first President of the Institution of Mechanical Engineers and was succeeded in due course by Robert, as supremo of this now famous organisation.

Bearing in mind that early railways were developed against a background of industrial need, it is not too surprising that the initial technology break-through to mechanisation took place outside London, but once this had happened and particularly after the Stephensonian transport vision had been accepted, then the pull of the capital city, its financial standing and the sheer size of its domestic market soon became dominant. Having established that the 'new' kind of railway, as exemplified by the L&M, really did work – in even more spectacular form than envisaged – all the groundwork had been done for a transport revolution to be sown. It only remained to be seen who would be first off the mark as far as London was concerned.

The first moves to link London with Birmingham by rail were made in 1823, so the economic need was clearly perceived at an earlier stage. A company was formed and, in 1824, Sir John Rennie was asked to survey a route. In 1826, he made his first recommendation, a route via Oxford and Banbury, but not much came of it at the time and in 1829, two separate possibilities were proposed, one via Oxford and another via Coventry (the former being, in effect, a re-working of Rennie's original proposals). Two companies were formed and they amalgamated in September 1830 to avoid wasteful duplication of effort. A month later, George and Robert Stephenson were appointed jointly as engineers, George previously having been advisor to the 'Coventry' supporters. It was not, however, until 1832 that a bill was deposited and read in Parliament – only to be thrown out by the Lords later that year.

This was hardly a promising start – nine years effort and a failed bill – and seemingly at odds with some of the assertions made earlier in this account; but was it altogether surprising? In 1823, the locomotive was still a primitive and relatively untried concept (one can hardly envisage a horse-drawn London and Birmingham system!) and even George Stephenson's other famous pioneer steam route, the Stockton and

Darlington Railway, was still two years into the future. Furthermore, even in 1832, the success of the new style L&MR was still not too widely appreciated, given the slow growth of perception and awareness at this time, save in a few circles. So, in the then contemporary context, the '100 mile plus' nature of the embryonic L&BR was probably too much, too soon.

There were, of course, quite a few vested land and canal interests to overcome as well, but only a year later, in 1833, a very different situation obtained. By this time, the L&BR proposal could be adjudged alongside that for another new trunk line, the Grand Junction Railway, which proposed to link Birmingham with the L&MR, thus in effect completing the through rail link from London to two of the biggest English industrial concentrations, the West Midlands and Lancashire.

The GJR could also trace its roots back to 1823 and it, too, did not really get off the ground until the L&MR had become tangible fact. Thereafter, the destinies of the L&MR, GJR and L&BR marched hand in hand and the L&BR and GJR bills (in revised form in the case of the former) both went into the Statute Book on 6th May 1833. History shows that the GJR opened first (in 1837), largely because of the generally easier engineering work involved, but that this took place without ceremony on the part of the company.

This was partly because the country was in mourning for King William IV but largely because the GJR could hardly come into its own until the L&BR was complete. So it was that when the latter finally opened throughout on 17th September 1838, the world's first truly mechanised railway from a country's capital city to its major regions became established fact.

So much for the historical background – necessarily condensed here, since much is already on record in far more detailed form – but what of the line itself? Its route is well known and its geographical nature has scarcely changed in any significant measure since its opening. The biggest subsequent changes took place quite early, mostly in the context of local railway development around Birmingham, but Robert Stephenson's famous alignment through most of its journey is

as valid today as it was in 1838. In a sense, this gives the line additional claim to fame for not only was it well conceived in terms of economic viability, it was also engineered to a standard which has stood the test of time. In this, it pioneered not only the building of trunk railways in general but also established many concepts which the modern road engineer is not afraid to copy, albeit with different materials.

Both the Stephensons were involved in 1830, but once the L&BR bill had received Royal assent, Robert was appointed engineer-in-chief. This may not have been unconnected with the fact that George was simultaneously involved with building the associated Grand Junction line from Birmingham northwards; the complete link to Lancashire was, until George resigned from the GJR contract, very much a family affair!

By the spring of 1834, Robert Stephenson had begun his great work, the first sod being cut at Chalk Farm, the site of the originally intended London terminus – see Chapter 2. Robert's task was, in many respects, a re-run of his father's Liverpool and Manchester, writ much larger. Almost everything was made subservient to easy gradients and gentle curve alignment but this meant considerable cost in terms of heavy engineering and earthworks. It has been calculated, though I know not by whom, that in building the L&BR, Robert Stephenson and his team shifted, in four short years, more material than did the ancient Egyptians in building the whole of the great pyramids of the Nile Valley. This may or may not be true but it set the pattern for most of Britain and much of the world too.

The location of the London terminus had, after some discussion, been agreed at a site near Euston Square which meant a severe climb out for a mile or so to Primrose Hill (to clear the Regent's Canal); this was somewhat at odds with the general Stephenson ideal. These were early days in steam railway history and the canny Stephensons generally preferred to take no risk in terms of gradients. History was to demonstrate that locomotives could tackle much steeper slopes than at first envisaged, but Robert Stephenson played it safe and chose to set out his line at a 1:330 ruling grade. In consequence, the unavoidable slope – 1:70 at its steepest point – of

the first mile out of Euston (Camden Bank as it later became and still is known), was at odds with his preferred choice. Therefore, just as George had done between Liverpool and Edge Hill on the L&MR, Robert too used cable haulage, with winding engines at Camden, to get the trains up to Primrose Hill. As an aside, for those who are not too familiar with North London's geography, Camden Town, Primrose Hill and Chalk Farm are all within a stone's throw of each other in railway terms and the three names have, by tradition, been used somewhat indiscriminately. This narrative will be no exception!

Beyond Primrose Hill, Stephenson could and did align his route with his preferred ruling gradient, but in doing so he had to pay due attention to physical geography as well as to economics, so this seems an appropriate point at which to introduce yet another of those factors with which the modern land transport engineer also has to contend, but which was first seen in major form with the L&BR. This is the interaction between the landscape and the line of communication together with the methods used by the engineer to solve it; the starting point is the nature of the railway itself.

In an ideal world, railways would be straight and level and, in terms of high speed communication, this is still the case. Any departures in terms of gradient and/or curvature tend to work against this ideal, so the aim of the engineer is to get as close as he can. However, at this point economics begin to intervene. To 'level' a railway through undulating countryside involves expensive cuttings and embankments (in extremis, tunnels and viaducts), so there is always a temptation to detour round them. The earliest artificial waterways of the late 18th Century, the so-called 'contour canals', are a good example of the same principle at work in a previous age. This then adds distance to the route with consequential extra costs in terms of time in transit, fuel and maintenance.

In the last analysis, the perceived economic role of a railway determines how much expenditure can be accepted to get close to the ideal. The economic need for the L&BR obviously put it into the category of a line which would justify good alignment but, in this case, there was a further factor, already touched upon, that of the locomotive itself. The Stephensons, it must be admitted, were more cautious than some of their near contemporaries as to the gradients which they considered locomotives could climb without too much adverse effect on their haulage capability. In consequence, simply to accommodate Robert Stephenson's 1:330 gradients, the engineering of the L&BR was probably more expensive than it need have been. Curiously enough, however, the consequences of this slightly cautious attitude have been advantageous to every succeeding generation of motive power.

Developments over the next ten years were to establish that something between 1:100 and 1:200 was a not unreasonable ruling grade for a high speed main line, provided curves were gentle and that, if need be, steam locomotives could quite readily tackle gradients far steeper than Camden Bank. In retrospect, therefore, Stephenson's approach may seem slightly quaint; but in the contemporary context it made much sense. Moreover, even fine engineers such as Joseph Locke who, in their pursuit of cheaper construction, took an *over* optimistic view of the power of steam locomotives to climb hills, left legacies such as the Lake District's Shap Bank in their wake – an operational nightmare until the onset of electrification in the 1970s. Balancing one extreme against the other, it seems reasonable to conclude that Robert Stephenson's solution was the better.

Now at this point – purely in the interests of objectivity – we must also mention that other famous engineer building a trunk line to London at much the same time: Isambard Kingdom Brunel with his Great Western Railway between London and Bristol. This line (the *second* trunk route to get into London by the way, 1935 and 1985 GWR celebrations notwithstanding!), was even less severely graded, for the most part, than Stephenson's L&BR, but in Brunel's case, local geography was generally on his side in the shape of the Thames Valley route. He therefore had fewer absolute problems to solve, but it is a matter of history that he too did things in the grand manner if he had to: Box Tunnel and Maidenhead Bridge for example. But Stephenson's problems were, on the whole rather more tricky.

Robert Stephenson was not the first engineer to tackle the business of putting a near straight and level alignment through rolling countryside. His father had done much the same on a smaller scale between Liverpool and Manchester while, in an earlier age, canal engineers such as Telford had also assayed the problem in such famous instances as the Shropshire Union Canal and the, still spectacular, Pontcysyllte Aqueduct on the Llangollen Canal. But Stephenson can still be given the prize for being perhaps the first engineer to conceive it on such a grand scale. Taking advantage of the geography where he could and tackling it with bold engineering where the landscape was less accommodating, he succeeded brilliantly. To appreciate his solution, we must look at that intervening landscape.

Between London and Birmingham, the underlying geological structure of England lies predominantly SW–NE, particularly in the shape of the Chiltern Hills (chalk) and the Cotswold Hills (limestone), but with other lesser ridges also aligned in parallel. These ridges are separated by often broad vales, predominantly of clay; so in general, the line of railway is, perforce, across the grain of a landscape which demonstrates a sort of ridge and furrow profile, writ rather large unless something is done about it.

Earlier forms of transport such as the Roman Watling Street (the origin of the modern A5) and the Grand Junction, later Grand Union Canal had to tackle much the same problems in much the same places, but then we can, perhaps, safely assume that the Roman Legions could march up and down hill (they did, at least, have a decent surface on which to do it) and that the canal user was prepared to face the time-delaying consequences of flights of locks. Stephenson's new railway was designed to be different. Speed was the essence of railway, then as now, and a modern transport artery, even in the 1830s, could not allow itself to be too inconvenienced by geography.

These considerations are, of course, fairly self-evident in our modern day and regularly witnessed in the form of new road construction, be it motorway or by-pass. The modern motor road is almost, if not quite as sensitive to grade and curvature changes as a railway and it no longer occasions much surprise to see hills removed or valleys in-filled to produce an appropriate alignment. But in the 1830s, nothing like this on anything like this scale had ever been seen before. It was, in truth, one of the technological marvels of the age and caused just as much interest and excitement in its own way as did the first manned space flights of a much more modern era. It certainly inspired a plethora of works by contemporary writers and artists, not the least being the famous series of Bourne illustrations of the construction of the line, some of which are reproduced in his book.

Before considering the engineering problems, one final point needs to be made. The L&BR was conceived as a single entity and in this respect was something of a paradox. Although it established engineering methods and ideas which others were to follow, it was one of relatively few long distance British routes which were actually planned as a homogeneous whole. There were, in fact, only five British instances where just one company built a line more than 100 miles in length under a single Act of Parliament[1]. Even below 100 miles, there were not too many planned long distance routes compared with those which were eventually formed out of 'end-on' amalgamations of somewhat more local concerns. Thus, although the Stephensons *thought* in terms of a national network, in reality it was achieved mostly by piecemeal methods and without central planning. Had the original L&BR concept been copied in strategic as well as engineering terms, we might well have had a rather better railway network in Britain, less vulnerable to competition, in the 20th Century.

However, no such considerations can have been in Robert Stephenson's mind when he embarked on his mighty concept. Having left Euston – a story in itself, see Chapter 2 – and surmounted the bank to Camden, the line struck off on its high speed alignment from Primrose Hill. Here impinged the first of the physical obstacles, the so-called 'Northern Heights' of the London basin, parallel to but south of the main Chiltern Hills and the reason for the first of Stephenson's engineering masterpieces, Primrose Hill Tunnel. Tunnelling was no new idea – the canals had done it for generations – but the outward manifestation betokened a new age. Not content with merely tunnelling the ridge, Stephenson gave its east portal a magnificent classical treatment whose symbolic

[1] Appleton: 'The Geography of Communications in Great Britain', OUP

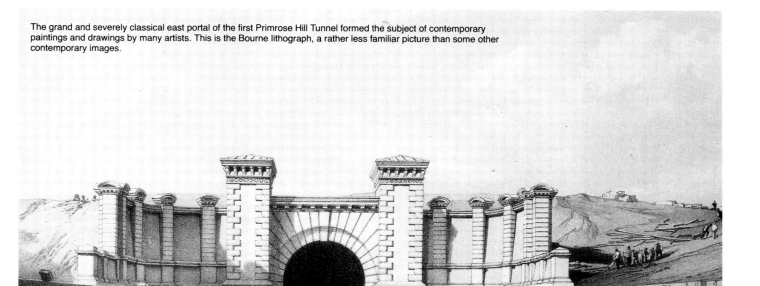

The grand and severely classical east portal of the first Primrose Hill Tunnel formed the subject of contemporary paintings and drawings by many artists. This is the Bourne lithograph, a rather less familiar picture than some other contemporary images.

'gateway' characteristics can surely have been no accident. Its severe symmetry, soot blackened, still greets the northbound traveller from Euston. Though now surrounded by much additional railway and urban development, it began its life amongst green fields.

This symbolism was, in retrospect, not only a flamboyant gesture of self-confidence and a means of retaining the land surface behind the tunnel mouth and to the sides of the approach cutting; it was also re-assuringly *solid*. In those pioneer days, rail passenger travel must have seemed to many a risky and dangerous sort of business and it certainly did not lack for detractors, especially the dispossessed stage coach operators who spared no opportunity to make much of the risks of locomotive boiler explosions and the like. Tunnels, in particular, may well have seemed fearsome things, creating as much apprehension to the new railway traveller as a first flight in an aeroplane can still do in our modern age. A tunnel portal which looked solid and substantial, moreover, one styled in a manner most reminiscent of the grand gateway to a stately home, must have gone some long way to contribute a suitable sense of permanence and reliability to the whole enterprise.

There was, in all conscience, more than a bit of this sort of thing in the structures of the 19th Century railways. They exuded self-confidence and permanence and the early pioneers set the tone for a whole generation. Some have called it 'over-engineering' in the context of modern structures. It is true that less was known then of the fundamental stresses which are present in bridges, embankments and the like than we know today, so there was an undoubted tendency to play things safe. But one cannot help remark that save for a very few and quite celebrated exceptions at the 'limits' of contemporary technology, railway structures of the Victorian age did

not fall into disrepair quite so quickly as do their modern motorway counterparts! Moreover, the self-same 19th Century structures on the L&BR are mostly still performing their original function some 150 years later, carrying far greater weights and stresses at far higher speeds than could ever have been conceived when they were built.

It is not, however, the intention of this account to make invidious comparisons between Victorian and late 20th Century civil engineering; it is merely to point out how significant was the work of those pioneers, working almost at the frontiers of their own contemporary experience, in establishing standards and ideas which have stood the test of time. Neither is it intended to give a feature-by-feature description of every single step on the way of the L&BR – that is on the contemporary record. Rather, it is thought most helpful to select a few examples of the way Robert Stephenson tackled his problems so as to demonstrate both the nature of the transport revolution he and his father had started and to show how far-sighted it can now be seen to have been.

Primrose Hill Tunnel is actually aligned more or less East–West, the line having made a gentle left hand turn at the top of Camden Bank from its more northerly course out of Euston. Having overcome Primrose Hill, Stephenson then elected to continue in this westerly direction for a few more miles before striking NNW for Birmingham. This added a mile or two to the route but also meant that the main SW–NE ridges could sometimes be tackled at more promising locations. Primrose Hill itself could not be avoided but by continuing the line westwards, the main extension of the Highgate–Hampstead ridge could mostly be skirted before the line began to assume its 'proper' direction after Kensal Green. This also had the merit of putting the new L&BR very

Kensal Green, 1948. The absence of smoke from the engine clearly shows the nature of the so-called 'tunnels' at this location – they are in fact merely 'cut and cover' features. The train, an empty carriage stock working headed by Stanier Class 5 XP 4–6–0 No.45676 *Codrington* is on the down slow line, which followed the alignment of the original 1838 main line. The new fast lines of the 1870s are on the right, while the third pair of running lines on the left were added to take the electric trains after the great Primrose Hill re-arrangements – see Chapter 2.

close to the projected line of the GWR north of Acton and would have facilitated the latter making use of the entry into Euston had this notion materialised.

Maintenance of the gradient as the line finally tackled the extension of the ridge at Kensal Green caused a deep cutting, none the less, which passed under the Harrow Road at a very oblique angle. It was, when completed, covered in – much in the fashion of the 'cut and cover' lines later to become familiar on the Metropolitan Railway – to form the so-called Kensal Green Tunnel, more accurately described as a covered way. After this, the route took off for Harrow and Watford on a generally rising trend for most of the way so as to overcome the next set of ridges.

Once again, Stephenson showed a fine sense of geography and practicality. At Harrow, he could take the line on generally lower ground between Stanmore Hill to the NE and Harrow Hill to the SW, but he could not entirely avoid the Oxhey ridge stretching SW from Stanmore; the 40ft deep Oxhey cutting was the result. Had Stephenson had his way, he would actually have gone round the SW side of Watford rather than to the NE, thus making use of the Gade valley and the somewhat lower lying ground at Grove and Cassiobury Parks, but influential titled landowners objected, thus

forcing rather more major engineering works at Oxhey and Watford. However, Stephenson turned necessity into virtue by using 372,000 cubic yards of material from Oxhey cutting to help build the equally necessary Watford embankment.

The rest of the material for this embankment, which more or less marks the end of the first climb out of London and swallowed more than 1,000,000 cubic yards in its making, came from another consequence of the unwanted diversion – the cutting and tunnel to the north of Watford. Stephenson finally resumed his preferred alignment in the vicinity of Kings Langley. Modern highway engineers and planners may well sympathise with his dilemma – 'plus ça change, . . . '

Watford Tunnel itself, cut through chalk with unconsolidated intermixtures of sand and gravel, was a sort of dress rehearsal for the even more difficult problems to be encountered at Kilsby. As well as presenting engineering difficulties, it also saw human tragedy. Ten men were killed by a sudden sand and gravel invasion through a gap in the chalk and a shaft had to be sunk to extricate their bodies; it was later converted into a ventilation shaft.

Mention of this catastrophe serves as reminder that, so far, little mention has been made of the tremendous human dimension which attended these great railway engineering

This turn of the century view at Willesden Junction from an original LNWR postcard shows a much more impressive place than when the line was first built. A northbound express waits in the down 'fast' platform.

The great size of the Watford embankment is well seen in this 1937 view of the 'Coronation Scot' headed by Stanier LMS streamlined 4–6–2 No.6224 *Princess Alexandra*.

Watford Tunnel under construction was drawn by J.C. Bourne in 1837 and makes a fascinating comparison with the same view about a century later when LMS Stanier Class 5 4–6–0 No.5360 was in charge of a lightweight express. Note the effect of one hundred years of tree growth.

works. The railway network of Britain was built by manpower and very little else save for horses, modest quantities of explosive where necessary and some use of simple powered machinery. It was not until late in Victoria's reign that transport engineers could contemplate using mechanically powered earth movers for their major works, the London extension of the Great Central Railway in the 1890s being perhaps the best known example. Prior to that, from the mid-1830s to the mid-1860s, the railway builders of Britain had put down some 10,000 route miles almost entirely by manual labour, with almost as much to come in the next 30 years. As a measure of the incredible speed of this achievement, it is perhaps only necessary to point out that in a similar 30 year period (1957–87), our modern mechanised age managed to build rather less than 2,000 miles of motorway!

The L&BR was the first spectacular example of the work of this 'Navvy Army' as it was to become known, nowhere better exemplified than between Watford Tunnel and the crossing of the main Chiltern ridge at Tring. The route went via Boxmoor and Berkhamsted, taking advantage of some favourable landforms and closely following the alignment of the older Grand Junction (later Grand Union) Canal. However,

Stephenson's preferred ruling gradient meant that even if he started it just north of Watford Tunnel (which he did) and continued unbroken for the remaining eleven or so miles (which he also did!), the ridge would still need to be crossed at some 50–60 feet below even its lowest point, not to mention the need to overcome quite a few smaller problems on the way. Of them, we can perhaps single out two for particular mention, both justly famous.

At Boxmoor, an embankment was required and at Tring, an even greater cutting. These were the most famed locations for the celebrated 'horse-runs' whereby excavated material was either taken to the embankment top or removed from the cutting floor by means of wheelbarrows attached to ropes which, in turn, passed over pulleys before being hitched to the horse. When the horse moved, the barrow was guided up a precarious narrow plank by one of the navvies who, clinging on as best he could, put his life and limb at risk every time he carried out the manoeuvre. Amazingly, there was only one fatal accident (amongst hundreds of spills) to be set against the fact that in Tring cutting alone there were 30 to 40 such runs in its 2 ½ mile length and some 1,400,000 cubic yards of material removed.

The famous "horse-runs" at Boxmoor and Tring were both drawn by Bourne in 1837 and give a vivid impression of the manpower involved in the building of this railway.

From Tring summit, the line descends gently for the next twenty miles or so, much as it had ascended for most of the previous distance from London, save for the brief respite at Watford. This descent starts by crossing the gentle countryside of the Vale of Aylesbury to Leighton Buzzard, at which point the next intervening ridge is encountered, the red sandstone and ironstone, much associated with this part of the Bedfordshire/Buckinghamshire border. Yet again, Stephenson showed his mastery of terrain. By bringing his line down from Tring on his favoured 1:330 for some seven miles, he was able to reach a height at Leighton Buzzard which enabled him to cut through the sandstone on an almost level alignment to Bletchley (for Fenny Stratford) and Wolverton. In this, he took advantage of a natural valley, that of the River Ouzel – also used by the Grand Junction Canal – but he was not right in the valley floor and, in consequence, some engineering work was required, including Linslade Tunnel, to overcome parts of the sandstone ridge.

It was (and still is in places!) handsome country in these parts and not without its historical transport significance. Towards the end of the undulating country between Leighton Buzzard and modern day Bletchley/Fenny Stratford, the line crosses the old Holyhead road (the modern A5) at a place called Denbigh Hall. This was a transfer point to road (for onward conveyance to Rugby) during the short period in 1838 when the bulk of the line was open, but not the vital central connection through Kilsby Tunnel. More important than this, however, and a few miles further north, the L&BR found itself in close juxtaposition with the Holyhead road (a mile or two away at Stony Stratford) and the Grand Junction Canal, which it crossed near a small and, at the time, rather insignificant little village called Wolverton. This place also happened to be roughly half way to Birmingham (52 ½ out of 112 ½ miles), cheap land was available and plentiful and there was a good water supply for locomotives; which fortunate combination of circumstances caused the L&BR quite deliberately to choose this spot for its 'Central Depot and Station'.

The rest, of course, is history. In 1838, Wolverton became the site of one of the first company owned railway works in the land – and undoubtedly the longest lasting, celebrating its anniversary too in the same year as the L&BR.

Denbigh Hall, the transfer point from rail to road until Kilsby Tunnel was completed in 1838, quickly descended into semi-obscurity for almost a century, but its fortunes began to revive with the motor trade of the 1930s. This view was taken c.1900. Believe it or not, that quiet road is the modern A5, now by-passed twice since the 1950s!

Immediately beyond Wolverton, the line – still crossing the grain of the underlying structure – encounters one of its biggest river obstacles, the Great Ouse. The valley itself can hardly be called spectacular at this point but at its lowest, it was some 50 feet below where Stephenson wanted his railway; the great 1½ mile Wolverton embankment was the result, interrupted at the actual river crossing by one of the largest viaducts on the line.

The Wolverton viaduct, when under construction in 1837, was a further example of the new railway building to come under the perceptive eye of J.C. Bourne. When the line was widened in mid-Victorian times, a second viaduct was built which exactly followed this style and was in effect grafted onto one side of it.

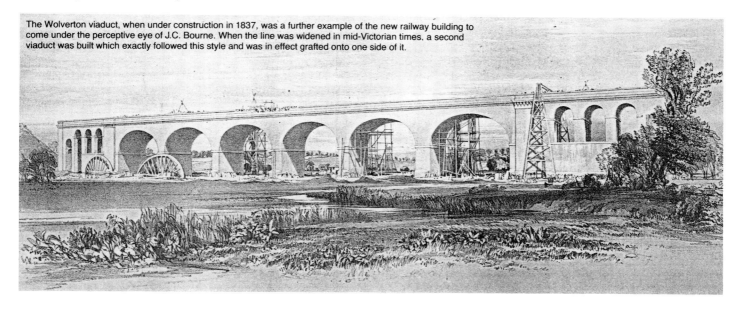

Stephenson's bridges were usually severely classical but he was an innovator. Two contrasting examples of his usual style are shown here (Nash Mill Bridge, King's Langley, incorporating wrought iron and a boldly conceived skew masonry bridge at Boxmoor) along with a somewhat more flamboyant, though structurally less taxing exercise at Rugby, presumably styled in mock Tudor to satisfy the aesthetic senses of the local citizenry. Interestingly, the latter was the only one to be replaced! All are, of course, illustrated from the famous Bourne prints.

Wolverton embankment was the largest on the line but so far, scant mention has been made of the bridges and viaducts on the L&BR. To be fair, subsequent railway builders were to construct far more daring and spectacular structures than those of this route, but in their time they were without parallel and they are mostly still there. Stephenson's structures were always boldly executed in a rather severe but classical style and he dared to innovate. Skew bridges, the imaginative use of iron in combination with masonry work and a simple boldness of concept were his hallmarks. Wolverton viaduct was and is as good as any one could instance, though there are many other contenders. At 220 yards long and 57ft from valley floor to parapet it was modest enough in size compared with some that followed, but it possessed a harmony of style and balance which has rarely been bettered.

From Wolverton to Coventry, the L&BR demonstrates features which were to become fairly characteristic of the complex interplay between geography and economics as the main railways developed. First of these was the by-passing of Northampton. This town stands on the Nene and to reach it, Stephenson would have had to descend a gradient steeper than 1:330, though in all conscience not too much steeper; even so, he ignored it, preferring instead to head through Blisworth on a near straight and level alignment and cross the Nene at Weedon, albeit at the cost of a huge cutting through soil and rock at Blisworth and a not insignificant embankment and viaduct at Weedon. He was, perhaps, influenced by the fact that at Roade (just south of Blisworth), a road connection was possible for Northampton, some four miles or so away. In the context of 1838, a road connection of four miles probably seemed acceptable and it was over 40 years before a loop line, taking in Northampton, was constructed between Roade and Rugby as an alternative to quadrupling the main line itself. Its quite gentle gradients are, none the less, greater than Robert Stephenson originally would have tolerated. Present day passengers heading through Roade (Blisworth) cutting cannot fail to notice the fall-away of the Northampton line in its steep-walled and cross-braced cutting to the east of the original route.

The second slight curiosity — for that seems the appropriate word to use — is the alignment from Weedon to Coventry. At Weedon, the line turns from a more or less SE–NW direction to an almost pure north–south alignment as it follows a small tributary of the Nene to the celebrated Watford Gap location. Here can be found juxtaposed some two millennia of transport history from the Roman Road (Watling Street) and its Bannaventa settlement via Buckby Wharf and Whilton Locks on the Grand Junction Canal to the line of the L&BR and the M1

'The Finest Permanent Way in the World' was the proud LNWR boast in its later years – and with some justification, but when the L&BR was built, its fine structures had to make do with somewhat more primitive track. This old LNWR postcard, though not of the L&B main line itself, shows somewhat similar track still in use at Winsford at the turn of the century.

motorway. For some miles, a less than half-mile wide tract of land embraces all four. Now Watford Gap is hardly the dominant physical feature which its name might imply but it has always been of major transport significance and no doubt Stephenson felt that where Romans and canal builders had gone, he too could follow. But in doing so, he was then forced into tunnelling through the Kilsby ridge to get to Rugby, thus giving himself by far his worst engineering headache – Kilsby Tunnel.

The curiosity arises from the fact that he chose to go that way at all! Furthermore, most contemporary and subsequent accounts of the L&BR concentrate on the formidable difficulties of Kilsby Tunnel without seriously addressing the question of why the line was there in the first place. Yet study of the surrounding landforms reveals that if, at Weedon, Stephenson had continued in a NW direction and stayed in the Nene valley until it peters out, he could have skirted just south of Daventry to Braunston on the Oxford Canal and could then have approached Coventry more or less parallel to the modern A45 with far less engineering problems on his way and saving a mile or so to boot. The writer has never seen any written analysis of the subject and it may indeed be that Robert Stephenson himself felt that the Watford Gap route was 'written in the tables', but somehow this seems a bit implausible given Stephenson's normal approach.

The Watford Gap route – vide Watling Street and the M1 – is actually rather more appropriate for traffic heading further north than for Birmingham and the West Midlands and the writer is inclined to believe that this is the key to the explanation. It focuses on the town of Rugby; Stephenson was, perhaps not just thinking of Birmingham when he laid out his line.

So far, this narrative has not strayed too far from the strict geographical limits defined by the title of the London and Birmingham Railway, but even as it was being built, things were developing quickly elsewhere and there was more than a degree of strategic thinking already at work. On the L&BR, it first reveals itself at Rugby. Here, the route was planned to be joined by the Midland Counties Railway to Leicester, Nottingham and Derby, thus making the London–Rugby stretch the common link in a rather larger scenario. Although the MCR decision was not actually made until 1836, it could well be that Stephenson had realised from the start that, in the national context, Birmingham was very unlikely to be the final destination. Indeed, the GJR, building simultaneously, was already destined to complete the link from Birmingham to Lancashire.

However, one does not have to study the map long to realise that Birmingham is not exactly on the direct or easiest route from London to Lancashire; that lies via the Trent Valley, and the logical jumping-off point is, yet again, Rugby. The Trent Valley cut-off from Rugby (L&BR) to Stafford (GJR) was in fact opened in 1847, only nine years after the L&BR itself; from then onwards (the two pioneer trunk lines were now both part of the larger LNWR, formed in 1846), Birmingham was by-passed by many of the principal northbound trains.

This LMS view of the north end of Rugby station was taken in 1947 and within six months or so, the railways were nationalised; but the train shed, signal box and signals themselves are all still firmly LNWR in style. The engine (Class 2P 4–4–0 No.543) is, however, ex-Midland and the second carriage is of Lancashire and Yorkshire Railway origin.

All told, therefore, Rugby seems to hold the key. Had it been viewed in the same sense as was Northampton in the early days (they were much the same size) then one feels the L&BR would have had no compunction in by-passing it and heading via Daventry to Coventry and Birmingham, the two most important places. It did not happen this way and in terms of future development it is just as well. Dare we, therefore, also award Robert Stephenson an extra credit for foresight to compensate for his at first sight rather strange choice of route via the Kilsby ridge?

Interestingly, 20th Century motorway development in the same area has witnessed what amounts to a virtual replay. The M1 was first 'billed' as the London–Birmingham Motorway. It went as far as Crick, just north of Watford Gap and although the M45 for Birmingham actually took off at the latter point, it could go *over* Kilsby ridge because of the somewhat less critical gradients on a motorway (1:30 desirable maximum). But, be it noted, it did keep south of Rugby and it did join the A45 route near Dunchurch. Very soon afterwards, the M1 became re-designated the London-Yorkshire Motorway (as had always been the intention) and the M1/M6 junction was opened a few miles north of Watford Gap. The M6 by-passes Birmingham to the north exactly in the manner of the line from Rugby to Stafford in 1847.

Stephenson can never have conceived of motorways but where he led, they eventually followed.

However, back to Kilsby Tunnel: while not the last of the engineering problems on the line, it was undoubtedly the most daunting and costly too, both in terms of lives (26 men killed) and money. The appointed contractor failed to meet his £90,000 estimate and the L&BR took over; it eventually cost £350,000. Progress was slow, hampered by water and quicksand and to cope with this delay, no fewer than 18 working shafts had to be sunk in a distance of less than 1½ miles. Some 1,300 men were continuously employed and it became the critical point which determined the opening of the whole route. Other horizontal shafts, parallel to the tunnel, were dug for drainage purposes, the water then being pumped to the surface, and two 60ft diameter ventilation shafts were also provided – surmounted at the surface by high brick walls whose crenellated parapets still dominate the surrounding landscape.

Perhaps the most interesting constructional feature was the use of powered machinery. Twelve stationary steam engines were used, day and night, mostly for pumping but some to raise and lower material, the latter being supplemented by horse-powered gins. Contemporary accounts were long on statistics and these, for their time, must have seemed well-

Above Trent Valley Junction has been the point of divergence for the principal northbound traffic since 1847, the L&BR continuing its independent way to the Midlands in the right foreground. This view shows the unique BR Standard Class 8P 4–6–2 No.71000 *Duke of Gloucester* heading north with the 'Mid-Day Scot' in September 1958.

Below Kilsby Tunnel was probably the most 'mechanised' of the construction sites and in these views, Bourne gives us great detail of the steam powered head gear for the main shaft and the steam pumps for draining the tunnel. The latter view also shows details of one of the several horse-powered 'gins' for lowering the workforce down the intermediate shafts.

nigh incredible: 1,000,000 bricks in the deepest ventilation shaft, 30,000,000 bricks overall and 172,000 cubic yards of material removed from inside the hill.

After Kilsby, the remaining 34 miles or so to Birmingham must have seemed mild by comparison, even though it represented almost one third of the whole route and was itself nearly as long as the whole Liverpool and Manchester line. There were, however, further interesting structures to note, not least the simple and gracefully stylish Avon viaduct between Rugby and Coventry and the delightful juxtaposition of the Blyth viaduct near Hampton in Arden alongside an old packhorse bridge, the scene being still here today.

And so, at last, Robert Stephenson brought his famous line into Birmingham, the last noteworthy structure (across Lawley Street and the River Rea) being the longest viaduct on the route, after which the line converged with the Grand Junction Railway from the north immediately before entering a terminus alongside that of the GJR at Curzon Street. It had taken only four years to build.

The Birmingham end of the L&BR has never been given quite as much attention as Euston and in this respect, this book does not depart from accepted custom. However, we can at least conclude this preliminary look at the line with an attempt to explain why.

Curzon Street Station was, in its own way, just as striking in its early days as Euston — the road entrance in this case being in the softer Ionic style rather than Euston's bold and severe Doric — and mercifully, the main station building is still 'in situ'; but in all other respects it sowed the seeds of its own destruction, being overtaken by events which were almost predictable even before the line was finished. Part of the reasoning has been given earlier during the discussion of the Kilsby Tunnel route, but even before the Trent Valley line was completed, the inconvenience of 'in and out' movements at what was, after all, only the half-way stage in the London–Lancashire journey must have been irksome. Furthermore, just as at Euston, the original ten acre site was far too constricted — in fact even more so by being almost full from the start and with an engine-house to boot — a matter made worse by the arrival of the Birmingham and Gloucester line in 1841 and the building of the Birmingham and Derby Junction Railway in 1842. This company first ran into Lawley Street Station, but its trains too began to use Curzon Street in 1845.

However, unlike Euston which was a genuine terminus, Birmingham was essentially a focal point of routes from different directions; in particular, it represented a crossing point between the London–Lancashire and Derby–Gloucester routes. Under these circumstances, there was little to be gained from having all four converging routes coming into terminal sites — far better to build a new and larger station which would allow through working. This was authorised in 1846 and duly came to realisation, along with a fair degree of re-alignment of approach tracks, in the form of New Street Station in 1854. It perhaps need hardly be stated that Robert Stephenson designed it. Even though through running between Derby and Gloucester did not become established at New Street until 1885, the old Curzon Street became a purely goods depot when New Street opened and the final part of the original L&BR approach to the city functioned merely as a goods spur off the new approach lines.

Like Euston, Curzon Street began to outgrow itself even before it was superseded by New Street station. Within a few years of the arrangement shown in Bourne's original lithograph, the L&BR had grafted a small hotel (the old Queen's) onto the left of the building and by the time the picture was taken in May 1947, Curzon Street had been a purely goods station for almost a century, the hotel itself had been converted to offices and there was a newer and much larger 'Queen's Hotel' near New Street.

Interior view of the old unloading platforms at Birmingham Curzon Street Goods depot taken on 2nd February 1932. They are believed to be the platforms added c.1841 for the Birmingham and Gloucester trains, the original L&BR platforms being on the right.

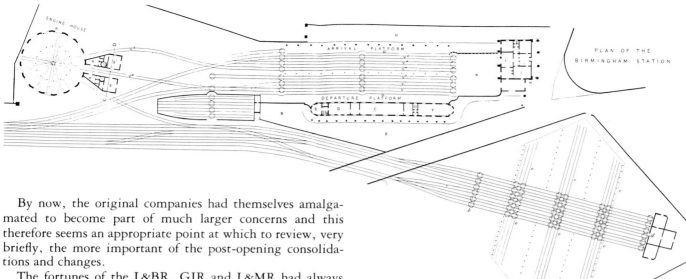

Original track plan of Birmingham Curzon Street Station showing a similar assymmetric layout to that adopted at Euston. However, in this case, there was no spare land available on the original site.

By now, the original companies had themselves amalgamated to become part of much larger concerns and this therefore seems an appropriate point at which to review, very briefly, the more important of the post-opening consolidations and changes.

The fortunes of the L&BR, GJR and L&MR had always marched hand in hand once the final link was forged south of Birmingham. This was taken to its logical conclusion in 1846, though not without a bit of acrimonious jockeying for position, when they, along with the Manchester and Birmingham (whose line actually ran only from Manchester to Crewe!), united to form the essential core of the new and soon to become mighty London and North Western Railway. In like manner, the Midland Counties (diverging from the L&BR at Rugby) and Birmingham and Derby Junction Railways were prime ingredients of the Midland Railway, formed in 1844, into which was absorbed the Birmingham and Gloucester in 1846.

The Midland and LNWR stood eyeball-to-eyeball at Birmingham (and elsewhere for that matter) for some three quarters of a century and the detailed history of their rivalry is well recorded already. It started off as collaboration in that the LNWR provided the link to London for both of them but soon, rivalry usually replaced co-operation (joint activities at Birmingham New Street notwithstanding) and it was ironic that they should be forced back together at the great railway grouping of 1923 when they became the two largest constituents of the new London Midland and Scottish Railway, to which company the L&BR route belonged when its centenary was celebrated in 1938.

By then as it has since remained, the original L&BR had been widened to four tracks along most of its length, stations have come and gone and most of the line is now only the first element of the principal route from London to the far north of Scotland. Some of these subsequent changes are recorded elsewhere in this book, but whether it be as a 'stand-alone' in the 1830s or the essential link in a much larger system, the first 80 miles or more of the L&BR have always been the spinal cord of the British railway network and as long as there are railways in this country, one suspects this will always be the case. The line was, indeed, a new form of transport link.

Birmingham New Street was hardly renowned for its charm or beauty, and in its modernised form is probably even less attractive, but like Euston it had character in steam days and, unlike Euston, was a fairly practical place from which to take a train. This view shows the LNWR side in mid-Edwardian days.

Chapter 2

THE EUSTON STORY

This once familiar view of the approach to Euston from the Euston Road can scarce be recognised today. Even though the lodges still survive, the statue of Robert Stephenson has been moved and a new rash of buildings has appeared 'to take over the 'masking' role once performed by the Euston Hotel in the distance. In neither case could the actual station be seen!

Within less than a mile length of the Euston Road there stand three of the most important terminal stations in British railway history. Two of them, Kings Cross (1852) and St Pancras (1868) still carry the visible evidence of that history in the form of their noble train sheds and, in the case of St Pancras, the even more flamboyant frontage of the Midland Grand Hotel, but of the original and most significant of them all, Old Euston, there remains nothing save the two small lodge gates, built in 1870, now fighting for survival and recognition amongst the concrete and glass of a century later. Behind them stands the New Euston, dating from the mid-1960s, always presuming that you can find it amongst the subsequent rash of office blocks and high-rise buildings which, as was the case with their 19th Century predecessors, are doing their best (and succeeding!) to hide the railway gateway to the North.

This modern day symbolism is more than skin deep and almost encapsulates the story of Euston station itself. It was and still is the oldest railway terminal in continuous use in a nation's capital city and many times in its history has paid the penalty of being the pioneer, but of its long-lasting significance there can be no doubt.

We left Euston with scarcely more than a mention at the start of the climb out to Primrose Hill, but its role and function were so much part and parcel of the general growth of railways that it is now necessary to have a look at it in rather more detail. From the very beginning it had its problems, not least those pertaining to where, exactly, it should be located.

The original intention was to locate the London terminus of the L&BR at Camden Town and the first contracts for the line were let out on this assumption. It was not long, however, before the directors felt it advisable to seek a site closer to the centre of the Metropolis. At that time, there was a degree of debate as to how far into London these new railways should be allowed to penetrate. As early as 1831, or thereabouts, sites in the vicinity of the Strand or Marble Arch are alleged to have been advocated and the unsuccessful 1832 bill proposed a terminus near Euston Square. The later and successful bill of 1833 fixed the site at Camden but one senses that this may have been a mere device to get things moving for, in 1834, land was indeed purchased in the Euston Square area and in 1835, a bill to extend the line to this location was successfully presented to Parliament. Subsequent events were to indicate that the line of the Euston Road and its westward extension were to be regarded as the limit of penetration by main line railways from the North of England – and the West too – as Paddington, Marylebone, St Pancras and Kings Cross all later bore witness.

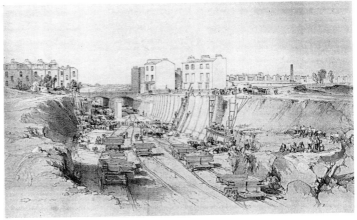

Above The tremendous scale of the works surrounding the linking of Euston to Camden Town is well captured by these fine Bourne drawings made in 1836 and showing, in close-up, the Hampstead Road Bridge and, in the wider view, the property demolition and excavations at Park Street. Below Further massive endeavour was needed at Camden Town both for the engine houses for the stationary winding engines and for the locomotive depot in the distance. Yet again Bourne has re-captured the tremendous human scale of the whole enterprise; one can scarce count the number of people in the picture. The alignment of the route itself is shown on the left as it curves towards Primrose Hill.

Notwithstanding the fact that 'the operations attending the *extension to Euston Square* rendered that an arduous and critical portion of the line', to quote a near contemporary account, Euston Station was itself opened for traffic, though still not complete in all detail, in July 1837, only two years after the extension bill had received Royal assent. In spite of the difficulties, one feels that the rapidity of its construction reveals that Euston was no sudden afterthought. Its final presentation to the public in the form of the celebrated Doric Propylaeum (to give it the proper nomenclature), certainly made a very positive statement of intent.

Euston and its approaches are best comprehended in two quite distinct categories: the station itself and the engineering and technical problems associated with linking it to the Camden Town area and thence to the main line. Since the form of the terminal facilities was largely determined by the needs and nature of the line itself, it seems best to start with the latter.

Every form of transport link has to reconcile the problems of its prime economic purpose with the constraints posed both by the land surface itself and the existing man-made structures. This, self-evident in our present age, was by no means unknown in the 1830s. From Euston to the Camden Town/Primrose Hill location is not much more than a mile, but the land rises all the way at an inclination far greater than could be overcome by Stephenson's favoured 1:330 ruling grade. Furthermore, between Euston and Primrose Hill, the Regent's Canal lies athwart the line of railway. The line could either go over it or under it. Stephenson chose the former course (a tunnel would have been wickedly expensive and very difficult to contrive), but this forced the 1:70/112/77 gradients which, even though the climb started as close to the terminus as possible, could not materially be improved. As an interesting aside to the same problem, the line to Kings Cross burrows under the canal (Gasworks Tunnel) and that to St Pancras, having crossed it by a bridge, stayed at what might best be called 'first floor level', thus putting the main passenger platforms well above the level of the Euston Road.

Having been forced to accept this sort of gradient, the line itself, even so, is mostly in cutting and such was the nature of existing development in this part of London that this cutting was crossed by no fewer than seven road bridges, some of which became far more widely known thanks to later generations of railway photographers. But that was not all. Stephenson, for reasons already touched on, was opposed to the use of locomotives on Camden Bank so he found it necessary to make additional provision for an alternative haulage system, over and above the facilities already envisaged for housing the locomotives which would be used on the main part of the route. There thus arose at Camden Town the infrastructure not only of what was to become the location of one of the most famous locomotive depots anywhere in the world, but also the provisioning of two stationary winding engines by means of which the trains could be cable-hauled from Euston to Camden.

The locomotives were housed on the arrival side of the line as it came out from Primrose Hill Tunnel and swung southwards for Euston, but the site was always restricted and eventually became intolerable. In 1847, a new shed for goods engines was built on the old site and another on the departure side for passenger locomotives. Interestingly, all that remains of the one time steam scene at Camden is the 1847 roundhouse

shed on the site of the original L&BR depot. It too was abandoned quite early, probably in the 1850s, and in 1865 was let to Gilbey's as a bonded gin store! It was later converted into a theatre, but at least it is still there! Meantime, the departure side site, which originally also housed carriage sidings and other facilities, was gradually developed exclusively for locomotives and by 1871, the whole locomotive depot was concentrated on the departure side of the line. Even so, 'Camden Loco' as a later generation was to know it, was always fighting for space, a problem which was, in steam days, never really solved to a wholly satisfactory degree.

Adding to the complications at this celebrated location was the fact that Camden Town was also the chosen site for the bulk of the freight traffic to the London end of the L&BR. The Euston extension did not affect this consideration, so Camden Goods (on the site of the original planned terminus) was simply given more space than it might otherwise have had. Even so, it still had to compete for space with the growing needs of the locomotive department on what was no more than a 30-acre site. In the context of the 1830s, this sort of space may well have seemed generous, but it soon became inadequate, largely because of the rapid expansion of freight traffic. Not the least of this expansion was that to the North London line which linked the L&BR with the docklands as early as 1851. This line took off to the north side of Camden Goods at Chalk Farm some half mile or so east of Primrose Hill Tunnel and headed off through Islington; it still does.

Camden Loco at the turn of the century displays an evocative assembly of LNWR locomotives of the Ramsbottom and Webb era. The main line to the north passes between the locomotive depot and the goods wagons outside Camden Goods on the right of the picture.

The net effect was to confine expansion at Camden Goods to the 'V' angle between the NL line and the main line to Euston, a space constriction which, at a very early stage, was a contributory cause of the later and extensive developments at Willesden, where there was more space, including enough for another locomotive depot used predominantly for freight. But it did not end there.

Stephenson had, wisely as it turned out, provided four tracks from the outset up Camden Bank in anticipation of the proposed entry to Euston of the GWR. In fact, this provision proved useful purely in terms of the 'home' team's needs. These additional running lines up the bank (hardly used at the start of the story) were soon brought into full use for LNWR 'fast' traffic and this eventually became manifest by the building of a second Primrose Hill Tunnel (to the south of the original bore) in 1879 and dedicated to these segregated 'fast' lines. At the same time, the original tunnel became the choice for 'slow' services, including, of course, the goods trains, after having seen a period prior to 1879 when all four running lines were interlaced through the original single tunnel.

Right to the end, Camden Loco was always cramped for space, very evident in this 'over the wall' picture of Stanier 4–6–2 No.46200 *The Princess Royal* tucked away on one of the back roads in late steam days, June 1962.

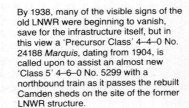

By 1938, many of the visible signs of the old LNWR were beginning to vanish, save for the infrastructure itself, but in this view a 'Precursor Class' 4–4–0 No. 24188 *Marquis*, dating from 1904, is called upon to assist an almost new 'Class 5' 4–6–0 No. 5299 with a northbound train as it passes the rebuilt Camden sheds on the site of the former LNWR structure.

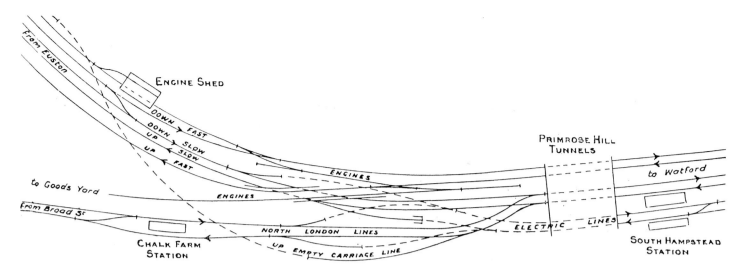

Diagrammatic representation, omitting some of the siding details, of the main running line re-arrangements at Chalk Farm consequent upon the building of the third Primrose Hill Tunnel and the installation of the complex flying and burrowing junctions.

Contractor's 0–6–0 saddle tank locomotive *Walsall* at work in 1903 during the widening of Camden Bank. Note the temporary 'lightweight' track for the removal of material by rail in pre-JCB days! The nearest wagon is lettered 'Firbank Ltd, London'. This area was to be occupied by the engine and empty carriage lines and can be seen in the left distance of the next view.

Setting aside minor changes, this 1879 arrangement remained more or less adequate until the late pre-grouping period when the LNWR embarked yet again on further augmentation at Camden Town/Primrose Hill. These works, started in 1915 but not finished until 1922 because of the Great War, involved the building of a vast complex of flying and burrowing junctions (to avoid conflicting movements) and a *third* Primrose Hill Tunnel. This arrangement is shown diagrammatically above and merits further amplification. It arose largely from the very nature of railway operating itself as it evolved over the years.

The L&BR's early development inevitably assigned it the role of pioneer in traffic handling as well as much else and nowhere was this more obvious than in the various changes on the approaches to Euston. The early decision by the GWR to go to Paddington, rather than Euston, undoubtedly eased the problem for many years on Camden Bank. Subsequently, the massive growth of traffic, not to mention a rapidly changing perception of what *could* be achieved, caused further changes.

Specifically, in the case of Euston, it was as early as 1844 that cable haulage up to Camden was abandoned in favour of locomotives and pretty soon afterwards, the desirability of segregating slow from fast traffic was appreciated. Camden Bank, as originally built, lent itself to this arrangement and it was not long before the main line itself was augmented progressively from two to three and then four tracks, mostly completed during the 1876–81 period. The 'doubling up' of Primrose Hill Tunnel to avoid the bottleneck between Camden and Willesden was part of this process.

Some twenty years or so later, further traffic increase forced a widening of Camden Bank itself to reduce congestion by allowing for separate engine and empty carriage roads to and from the terminus. This was completed c.1905, in consequence of which, the final convolutions a decade or so later at Primrose Hill were somewhat inevitable. In these, the aim was to alter the preferred 'country' disposition of two fast lines alongside two slow lines to a terminal arrangement which had departures on one side and arrivals on the other. This involved

Camden Bank in LMS days some 30 or more years later in 1938 and looking in the opposite direction from the picture on the previous page. No. 4 signal box (sometimes known as the Euston Carriage sidings signal box), from which the previous picture was taken, partly conceals the rear coaches of the down 'Coronation Scot', seen departing behind streamlined 4–6–2 No. 6221 *Queen Elizabeth*. Stanier 'Jubilee Class' 4–6–0 No. 5563 *Australia* is backing out from Euston on the down empty carriage line – see diagram page 30 – and the up side carriage shed is behind the streamliner. Most of the 'furniture' is still firmly LNWR.

carrying the 'up' (London-bound) fast line over the slow lines, arranging for empty carriages (from the slow line side) to be taken to and from the terminus without fouling the main running lines at all and further refined, on the 'in for a penny, in for a pound' principle, so to speak, by segregating the new electric suburban services from both Euston *and* the North London line onto a third set of independent running lines in the Chalk Farm area.

This final objective was achieved by building a third Primrose Hill Tunnel, this time to the north of but at a lower level than the original bore, linked to both the NL and Euston electrified slow lines by further burrowing junctions. This third pair of lines emerged from the new tunnel at South Hampstead and continued as an independent third set of running roads as far as Watford. Bakerloo tube trains join this electrified route at Queen's Park and the electrics cross from the 'up' to the 'down' side of the main fast and slow lines by means of a burrowing 'tunnel' south of Wembley. Beyond

Before and after scenes looking towards Euston at Park Street Bridge, further up the bank, taken in 1903 and c.1960 respectively. The new engine and carriage relief lines, on which stand Stanier 'Class 5' 4–6–0 No.45256 and 4–6–2 No.46247 *City of Liverpool* are seen under construction on the right of the first view.

The up fast fly-over at the top of the bank is seen here on 7th July 1954, being negotiated by the 'Shamrock' express headed by Stanier 'Princess Class' 4–6–2 No.46204 *Princess Louise*

This fine view of Camden Bank was taken between Park Street Bridge and the top of the hill on 22nd May 1949. The train is a down excursion headed by Class 5 4–6–0 No. 45418.

Out in the 'country' north of Wembley and Harrow, further widening (which also affected Euston) took place on the down side of the main lines. In this view at Headstone Lane the so-called 'new' lines, which were also electrified, are see in the foreground, while a northbound express headed by LMS Compound 4–4–0 No. 1152 gets into its stride on the down fast line.

Northchurch Tunnel, between Berkhamsted and Tring was widened in the 1870s by means of two new single bores. The new portals had brick facing rather than Robert Stephenson's favoured stone, though a happy attempt was made to harmonise the architecture. This view shows a southbound express on the up fast line behind 'Jubilee Class' 4–6–0 No.45741 *Leinster*.

Harrow, they made an end-on link to the original 'new' lines which had been added on the 'down' side for suburban steam trains in 1913. The first electric services (tube stock, as it transpired) arrived in 1917 and the full Primrose Hill scheme was effective, as stated, in 1922.

This massive amount of progressive rebuilding and alteration – there were very few periods of any significant length when something was *not* happening between 1840 and 1920 – would, superficially, appear to betoken inadequate planning in the first place, but this assessment would be unfair to Stephenson and his contemporaries. The fact is that the sheer success of the railway attracted traffic of a nature and volume which could scarcely have been conceived at the time of its building; the L&BR was, in effect, a victim of its own success. It is, in fact, a measure of Stephenson's genius that the original alignment never needed to be changed in any significant way, save for widening, and is still in use today. The only

noteworthy exception, apart from the deliberate deviation of the 1913 'new' suburban lines through Watford town centre, was an equally deliberate but rather more far-reaching deviation between Roade and Rugby. Here the second pair of lines, consequential upon the general widening, was deliberately taken via Northampton to improve facilities at that previously by-passed town. And although we have now strayed quite some way from Euston and Camden Town, it is important to understand both the scope of and reasons for the enlarged capacity of the L&B main line if one is to make any sense at all of the incredible convolutions which took place at Euston Station itself during the same period.

The L&BR was a trend-setter; where it led, others could follow and, if wise, try to avoid the mistakes which are the almost inevitable lot of the pioneer. Nowhere was this more apparent than at 'Old Euston', the first London terminus and arguably one of the least 'fitted for purpose' terminal stations

The Northampton 'deviation' line rejoins the main alignment of the L&BR at Clifton Road Junction south of Rugby, seen here in early BR days with a London bound express passing below the 'down' Northampton line and heading for the 'old' route via Weedon. The train engine is 'Jubilee' Class 4–6–0 No.45586 *Mysore*.

of all time! Even with the benefit of knowing why, it is still surprising that it survived, somehow or other, until 1963. Logic would have decreed its complete rebuilding at least half a century earlier and indeed this was thought about more than once. What is certain is that its fundamental inadequacy was apparent from such an early stage that few other railways copied it – which is undoubtedly why Kings Cross and St Pancras remain 'in situ' much as they have always done. Euston mostly showed the world what *not* to do, save for two quite magnificent exceptions, now, alas, gone.

To be fair to Euston, when it was built, no-one had any real idea what a big city railway terminus should look like, nor how big it should be, nor how large it might grow. The original Euston made a stupendous attempt to meet the first of these three criteria but, ever afterwards, was always striving to keep up with the consequences of the other two which, in time, eventually managed to submerge if not quite destroy the first. This latter criterion was the cause of the 'magnificent exceptions' alluded to in the previous paragraph: the famous Doric Arch and the equally famous Great Hall.

First, however, it is important to appreciate that almost from the start and for all its many faults, Old Euston was possessed of immense character, in large part probably due to the fact that it carried within it visible evidence of most stages of its, often chaotic, evolution. But the character was real enough and the public outcry which greeted its destruction in 1962 should not be confused with the modern kind of bleating from a lunatic fringe with only its own personal axe to grind; it was deep-seated and genuine. Old Euston was no mere icon, and with its passing, something important went with it.

The original Euston was conceived against a background of much contemporary confidence which contained, in hindsight, considerable naivety. There seems little doubt that the original site (only half-filled when the trains first ran) was considered more than adequate since the vacant space was confidently expected to be used by the GWR. This line was intended to join the L&BR near Kensal Green and use the second pair of tracks already planned down Camden Bank. For this reason, the symbolic gateway was placed, not central to the L&BR platforms but between what were expected to be two, rather similar, side-by-side facilities. Had it turned out that way, Philip Hardwick's magnificent Propylaeum would have completed a majestic symmetry. As it was, events began to change the outlook scarcely before the first mortar dried.

It was, however, the arch itself and its flanking pavilions, which first caught the popular fancy. The 'Gateway' symbolism was quite deliberate and the use of Yorkshire stone may well have been no accident either – after all, not only was this the new-style 'Gateway to the North', it was largely being masterminded by Northerners as well. In its architecture and in its function it stood like a gauntlet thrown down into the

The true symbol of Euston: Hardwick's famous propylaeum seen from the road access archways under the Euston Hotel c.1928.

hitherto largely unsullied South by 'Industry', here represented by the mechanical artefacts of the mostly Northern-based Industrial Revolution. The author can claim no real originality for this rather picturesque analogy, but he can at least agree with it. Industry was here to stay, said Euston, and London might just as well get used to the idea!

London did get used to the idea – very quickly – and profited handsomely in consequence, so any perceived affront which may have been caused by this blatant piece of Northern architectural propaganda (not that there seems to have been too much objection at the time) was very soon mollified by the considerable commercial benefits which the railway brought with it. And therein lay Euston's eventual downfall. Like the L&BR main line itself, Euston fell victim to its own success, but even more so. It was simply too small, a fact which became apparent from an early stage and it is no small tribute to its early owners that somehow or other they managed, repeatedly, to keep squeezing quarts into pint pots. Eventu-

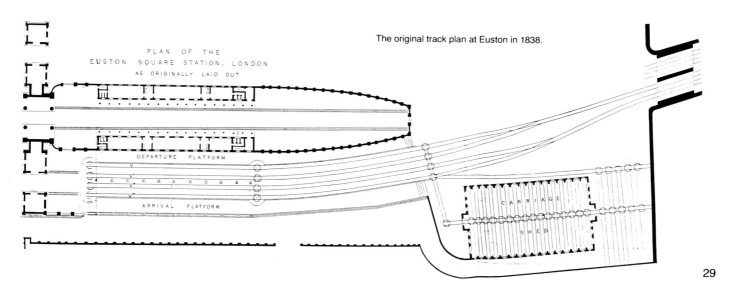

The original track plan at Euston in 1838.

PLAN OF THE
EUSTON SQUARE STATION, LONDON
AS ORIGINALLY LAID OUT

DEPARTURE PLATFORM

ARRIVAL PLATFORM

CARRIAGE

SHED

ally, of course, it involved more land acquisition and peripheral property demolition and produced ever increasing confusion and complexity, but somehow or other the essential character of the old place always managed to survive and one could actually quite get to like it!

The first visible changes took place within a year of opening and provided a first hint that the splendid prospect of Hardwick's arch from the south was not sacrosanct. Ever mindful of the advantages of earning an honest extra penny or two, the fledgling L&BR obviously reckoned that travellers would welcome a place in which to rest overnight either before or after long journeys. Accordingly, on either side of Euston Place, immediately in front of the pavilions flanking the Propylaeum, were built two hotels. More properly, that on the east side was the only one which qualified as a hotel, the western building being more of a dormitory. Together they were known as the 'London and Birmingham Railway Hotel and Dormitories' and came into use in 1839/40. Unwittingly, perhaps, the L&BR had pioneered the modern hotel industry.

The enterprise was growing like a rampant vine and, even before the hotels were opened, the L&BR had built a new office block at the corner of latter day Drummond and Cardington Streets. No doubt it was needed but it effectively hampered any symmetrical extension of the station itself beyond the originally designated 'GWR' area. By now, of course, the GWR had decided on its own independent London terminus which was just as well, for as early as 1840, extra platforms were needed at Euston in order to cope with new L&BR traffic now feeding to and from the line from the Midland Counties Railway at Rugby. These new platforms were built on the 'GWR' side of the original site but, for some reason, were not made symmetrical with the original ones. The rot had set in! Known as the 'York' (by reason of the destination of some of the trains which first used it) this new platform was on the extreme NW corner of the original site and later became Platforms 9/10 in the final pre-1963 version of the station. From this point onwards, for ease of identification, the platform numbers of this final version of the old station will be used for reference purposes. On this scheme, what was left of the two original platforms — not much more than their alignment in fact — became Nos. 5 and 6.

By this time, it was clear that Euston's role as a terminus was destined far to exceed the original ideas. The Midland Counties link would become but the precursor of the many more speedy developments during the 1840s. The Chester and Crewe line of the GJR opened in 1840 and the Chester and Holyhead (for the Irish traffic) would duly extend it to the Welsh coast in 1846 and to Anglesey itself by 1850. The Trent Valley route (by-passing Birmingham) was destined for opening in 1847, thus giving direct through services to Lancashire, while the County Palatinate was to find itself linked to Scotland by rail in 1848. By 1850, shortly before the opening of Kings Cross, Euston would become the London rail head for all traffic to the North of England and Scotland and, as early as 1846, it had girded its loins in anticipation of most of these new expansions.

By this time, the newly formed LNWR was in charge and, accordingly, even before its Trent Valley and Scottish links were completed, the new company embarked on the second really grandiose phase of Euston's evolution, the massive central administrative block, designed to cope both with existing overcrowding at the station and to accommodate future expansion in terms of passengers and office staff. Built in 1846–7, it was placed between the 'York' and the original platforms. It virtually filled the whole of the available space, it was off-centre in relation to the Doric Arch and it torpedoed any further hope of a rational development of the site in terms of train movements and platform additions. It was in every respect the right sort of building and in almost every other respect it was in entirely the wrong place! But it contained one majestic compensation and one minor architectural masterpiece: the Great Hall and the Shareholders' Meeting Room.

These two splendid chambers, like the whole block, were designed by another Philip Hardwick, this time the son of Stephenson's chosen architect for the original station some ten years earlier; and the Great Hall itself represented a whole new conception of travel. History does not tell us what Hardwick felt about the early ruination of his father's planned symmetry

The final track plan of Euston and its approaches before the 1960s modernisation.

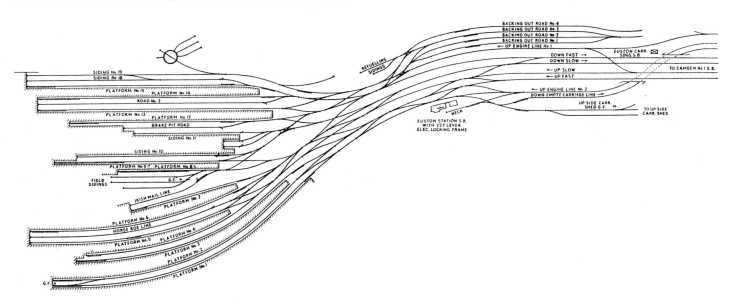

but his Great Hall was even more impressive than the Propylaeum, almost as if to apologise for being in the wrong place. It was and remained the largest waiting room in the British Isles for more than a century and in spite of many later additions of an inappropriate nature, the LMS enquiry bureau of 1930 in the centre being particularly tasteless, it was never really overshadowed in its overall splendour.

The Shareholders' Meeting Room was, if anything, even more of a jewel. Approached by a truly memorable staircase at the north end of the Great Hall and with its entrance door surmounted by a bold bas-relief statue of Britannia and her lion supporters (the LNWR 'heraldic emblem', also found on the company carriages, its locomotives and even its stationery), the room's proportions were nigh-on perfect and, perhaps, built to a slightly more human scale. The pity was that more did not see it for it was, essentially, a 'non-public' room. Along with the Great Hall, this room has oft times been described in detail and to repeat the substance here would savour of plagiarism, but before leaving them, it seems to the writer that their significance, particularly that of the Great Hall, have had less than their due share of attention.

Grandly designed rooms were no rarity in Victorian England – they were almost *de rigueur* for any organisation worth its salt from Town Council to Railway Company – but a railway waiting room on this gigantic scale (it had the largest flat-panelled ceiling in the world) was something quite new and remarkable. Never mind that it may have been sited wrongly, its message was clear. Travel was now perceived as being for everybody rather than a privileged few. The grand station assembly room had replaced the small smoke-filled and rather exclusive parlour of the stage coach inn, and the mere fact that a railway company was prepared to spend,

possibly even in excess, to demonstrate its goodwill to all its potential patrons, spelled out its own psychological message.

Speaking from personal experience of using the Great Hall, it somehow made the passenger feel important, even in its final years. Moreover, there was an almost implicit promise of commitment in the mere concept which has most certainly not transmitted through to its modern day replacement, nor for that matter to its modern day imitator, the airport terminal. Their sole function seems to be to provide a clear open space through which one is encouraged to pass as quickly as possible without getting in the way and certainly without any thought of enjoying the experience! The Great Hall was actually a welcoming sort of place for all its hugeness and one could actually enjoy simply sitting there. That its promise of commitment seemed to become rather eroded in its later years was no fault of the room itself. It was the first grand gesture made to ordinary people by a brand new railway, the LNWR, and it set the tone for much which followed on this, soon to become famous, system. As if to set the seal of approval on the whole endeavour, the LNWR, in 1852, four years after his death, erected a statue of George Stephenson at the foot of the grand staircase to the Shareholders' Room.

The Great Hall promised much and for the most part it was justified. Interestingly, however, no other British railway quite copied this famous room, even though the message it proclaimed was taken up enthusiastically by many of them. By the time most other railways were ready to make their own 'London' statements, the lessons of Euston had already been learned and most of them went more for the grand 'train sheds' – the 'Great Victorian Railway Cathedrals' as some have described them – which were often accompanied by splendid facades, regularly associated with palatial hotel accommodation. In this sort of development one can perhaps see something of the L&BR influence, but Euston's cathedral was its Great Hall. It was never copied in Britain but its influence was great.

The Great Hall and its 'en-suite' rooms and offices were, without doubt, the right sort of provisioning for the growing Euston but their somewhat unfortunate location eventually caused the station to be divided into three parts, a situation from which the place never subsequently recovered. But this was in the future and before incipient became real disaster, it was decided that a better entrance from Euston Road was the first priority, giving direct access to the main east—west road artery. Here, at least, some symmetry was achieved. During 1869–70, a road was driven in direct line with the Propylaeum straight through Euston Square Gardens and, at the Euston Road end, a pair of handsome classical lodges were erected; between them was a statue of *Robert* Stephenson, who had died in 1859 at the relatively young age of 56. These two lodges and the statue (now relocated to an open space in front of the new station) are all that survive at Euston of the whole pre-1963 complex.

Between 1870 and 1880, one could get quite a good view down Euston Grove between the hotels to the Doric Arch and, had things been left that way, the approaches to Euston at least might still have been acceptable, but it was not to be. In 1881, the two hotel blocks were linked by a not wildly exciting looking in-fill building with no more than poky little carriage arches at ground floor level to allow road traffic through. Euston Hotel had arrived at its final form – and it was not a bad hotel, all things considered – but Hardwick's arch was hidden for ever.

So much for the approaches to Euston, what of the station itself? For a generation or so, the 'York' platform was the only addition to the original scene; it was not enough. More or less coincidental with the completion of the new carriageway approaches from Euston Road, enlargement of the station itself was well in hand. This took the form of building new arrival side platforms to the east of the original station, on land previously occupied by houses fronting onto Seymour (later Eversholt) Street. To do this involved demolishing the original carriage shed which was becoming more and more of an operational liability with its multiplicity of fixed-length and not very large turntables. Willesden south shed replaced it in 1871.

The new platforms, which became Nos. 1 and 2, were brought into use in 1871–3, along with a new cab entrance from Seymour Street which came into the station at the north end, crossing over the new platform tracks as a semi-spiral ramp leading to a bridge, from which it then descended alongside the new No. 2 platform, finally emerging onto Drummond Street to the east of the original Hardwick pavilions. This became the principal cab exit from the arrival platforms till the very last days of the old station. The new platforms were roofed over in a style matching the originals

The fully developed 'arrival' side at Euston seen from the top of Euston House in 1962, just prior to the demolition contractors moving in. The remnants of the original train shed are immediately in front of the buildings on the left, much modified by later additions.

but the roof itself was set some six feet higher. The whole of the older existing roof was then raised to match it by jacking up each pillar simultaneously in an extraordinary feat of 'ad hoc', yet enterprising, structural engineering which was carried out in just one week. Ever afterwards, the bottom six feet or so of the roof support pillars alongside Platforms 5 and 6 bore witness to this remarkable achievement.

Thus far, there were still only the 'York' platforms on the 'wrong' side, so to speak, of the Great Hall building, but traffic was still growing rapidly in spite of the fact that Euston had long since ceased to be the jumping-off point for trains to the Midland Railway or the NE of England. In particular, local traffic was now building up. This had not been much of a problem in the earlier days, indeed the company itself had done very little to encourage it compared with its promotion of long distance services, but by the early 1880s, pressures were growing.

Although the new 1871–3 platform was a considerable help, there was now nothing for it but to expand to the west of the site between Cardington and Drummond Streets and also examine the possibility of further enhancement on the arrival side. Thus, between 1887 and 1892, Euston saw its biggest expansion of platform facilities, more than doubling the previous quota. During this period, five new platforms (Nos. 11–15) were brought into use on the west side land; at the same time, a rather narrow double sided timber platform (Nos. 4 and 5) was puckered in somewhat uncomfortably on the arrival side, alongside and to the west of the new cab entrance from Seymour Street. The new west side platforms were separately roofed and given their own booking office and

Old Euston may have been chaotic but it had its own beauty, particularly under the curved canopies on the arrival side. These views of Platforms 4 and 5 were taken in 1939 and 1962 respectively. The LMS view, looking north and featuring the ex-LNWR Oerlikon electric train, clearly shows the original wooden construction of these two extra platforms – see text; by BR days, some degree of refurbishment had taken place but they were always rather narrow. On the BR picture, the end of the cab ramp from Seymour (Eversholt) Street can just be seen on the extreme left.

The new departure platforms at Euston could be hard to find and were a good deal less gracious than the earlier structures. However, this c.1934 LMS view, looking towards the platform barriers, looks quite neat and tidy and shows a fine array of both ex-LNWR and LMS standard carriages, including one of the famous clerestory diners – see Chapter 3.

cab entrance off Drummond Street, this time well to the west of Hardwick's pavilions.

This development effectively split the station into three distinct parts, a situation which remained unaltered in its basic configuration from 1892 to 1962! The arrival side (Platforms 1–6) had its own cab rank from Seymour Street, the new departure side (Platform 11–15) also had its own road approach, while between these two zones was a sort of hidden 'no-man's land', mostly tucked away behind the Great Hall and fed by road from what was left of the orignal courtyard behind the Propylaeum! This middle zone was much used for parcels and similar traffic, particularly Platforms 7 and 8, but by no means exclusively. Furthermore, strict arrival and departure segregation between the two peripheral groups of mostly longer platforms was by no means consistent. While Nos. 11–15 were, more or less, confined to departures, No. 6

was often similarly used – most notably perhaps during Edwardian days by the celebrated 2pm 'Corridor' train to Glasgow and Edinburgh – while Platform 2 was the regular *departure* platform for the West Coast Postal, simply because of its easy access (for road mail vans) via the Seymour Street cab drive.

One certainly had to *find* one's train at Euston!

Approaching the turn of the century, in 1899, the LNWR at last devised a scheme of complete reconstruction which envisaged bringing the whole station forward to a new frontage on Euston Square; an enormous project which, had it been carried out, would probably have involved the demolition of the Great Hall and the Doric Arch. It came to nought, as did some other ideas and the only really new feature was the arrival of the deep level tube lines (nowadays the Northern Line of London's underground system) and their associated

The changing face of Euston's trains in the steam era is well caught by this trio of views spanning some 60 or more years. The evocative LNWR view c.1900 shows the 10.00am departing behind a Webb compound 4–4–0 from what was to become the main arrival side of the station; the LMS picture shows a newly arrived express in 1936 behind 'Patriot Class' 4–6–0 No.5533 *Lord Rathmore* while the BR vintage picture shows the arrival of 'The Caledonian' at Platform 12 on the *departure* side, c.1960! The engine was, symbolically, the last of the Stanier 4–6–2s, No.46257 *City of Salford*.

surface entry points, most of which simply added to the clutter and made the business of getting round the station with any facility even more bewildering. The Great War brought all prospect of further changes to a halt.

Thus it was that the LMS (in succession to the LNWR after the railway grouping of 1923) inherited a station whose form had been 'set' in 1892 and which, even then, was less than satisfactory. Some desultory changes were made, including quite a bit of essential platform lengthening along with a thoroughly objectionable information bureau which, try though it might, could not destroy the magnificence of the Great Hall where it was, most inappropriately, located. But eventually, the LMS too resolved on a major reconstruction whose design, in the event, turned out to be a sort of Art Deco re-working of the LNWR's late Victorian cornucopia of 1899. It too would have involved the destruction of the Great Hall and Propylaeum but, like its predecessor, also failed to get built, this time because of the Second World War.

Part of this development was a much needed new Head-quarters office block and this edifice did at least arise alongside Seymour Street. This was and still is 'Euston House' and its Odeon-like exterior gives some sort of clue as to what parts of the LMS 'New Euston' might have looked like. Judging from contemporary drawings, the rest would have been a sort of

visual cross-breed between two 1930s buildings of some quality which did get built. One of them was actually an LMS creation, the Queens Hotel in Leeds and the other is the University of London Senate House. The LMS version of Euston might not in fact have been too bad and would certainly have typified the architectural mores of the day. In that, it would at least have been true to the spirit of Stephenson and Hardwick – and there was even talk of saving the old Propylaeum by moving it elsewhere on the site.

Whether one likes the style or not, Euston House was a very good example of its architectural period. It was extensively re-modelled inside prior to the BRB adopting it as its HQ building in 1986 and, regrettably, appears to have lost most of its 'in period' interior character in the process, but then one might have expected that, given the previous track record at Euston!

At the time it was built, however, it was sorely needed. By then, just about every property in the vicinity of Euston had been commandeered for railway office use and almost every available open space filled in with the most appalling mixture of buildings imaginable. The noble Propylaeum, fighting for space with its neighbours and surrounded by much tat, was only really visible – and then not particularly well presented – from Euston Place and its overlooking hotel rooms.

The heterogeneous clutter of buildings surrounding Hardwick's arch at the close of the old era, 1962, gives some clues as to why the rebuilding was overdue.

This was Euston in its final steam years and as many will still remember it. The place was, of course, hopelessly impractical and no-one can seriously argue with the BR decision to come to grips with the problem, but somehow one feels that a great opportunity was missed and that the BR attempt, following on the unsuccessful projects of the LNWR and the LMS was actually a case of 'third time unlucky'!

New Euston arose during the mid-1960s but it was hardly a case of 'Phoenix-like from the ashes'. The track layout was at last made sensible, the all-electric environment had, for all

practical purposes, levelled Camden Bank, and one could actually find the trains! The concourse itself was clean, as indeed was the station as a whole, and its spacious lofty nature was obviously meant to hark back to the old Great Hall. Even the refreshment rooms and coffee bars were actually more agreeable than those recalled from former days. But something was missing: the new Euston offered no sense of history at all. It was a child of the 1960s – a time when it was considered effete to admit that tradition and history had any place in modern thinking and, sadly, Euston became a 'non-

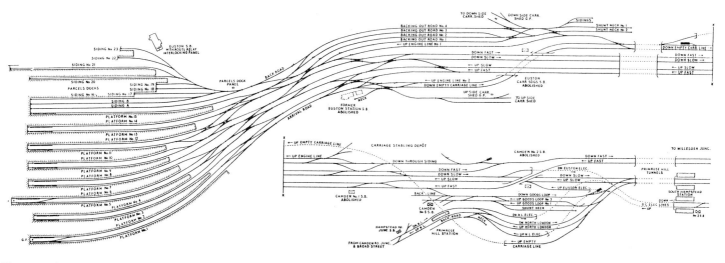

The new and vastly more rational track layout of the modernised Euston and its approaches from Primrose Hill.

The untimely death of a famous station. The pictures hardly need captioning but they show: demolition of Euston Hotel (the propylaeum behind it has already gone), breaking up the stones of the Euston Arch, the last rite of the Great Hall and the old heart of Euston completely ripped out. 'What shall it profit a man . . . ?'

place' in consequence. True, a slight attempt was made to pay lip service to the old order. Britannia was moved from her place of honour over the Shareholders' Meeting Room door to reside (for a few years) on a wholly unsuitable plinth in a wholly inappropriate place – the refreshment room. This nonsense of conscience was, happily, brought to a close a few years ago when she was despatched to the National Railway Museum where, one hopes, she might ultimately be as sympathetically re-displayed as is the statue of George Stephenson from the Great Hall, now standing symbolically overlooking a display of the events which happened before he came on the scene. Only Robert Stephenson on his plinth is given any real place of honour at the new station.

The Euston Road Lodges have been left alone but the scene behind them is just as 'tacky' as its predecessor. No sooner had the new Euston been completed and the area in front cleared of clutter than the greed of man and the accountants of BRB saw fit to erect a jungle of slab-sided office blocks of such monumentally boring aspect that they are every bit as bad as the mish-mash of assorted buildings they were designed to replace. It was a total replay of the in-filling of the old Euston Hotel, but what is really most galling is that whereas the old order had mostly evolved by accident out of necessity, this new lot was put there by design! Maybe the new Euston will never be a prime candidate for the architectural award of the year but at least, if anyone had really cared, they could have ensured that the new station stood revealed from Euston Road as some sort of symbol of the re-born modern railway, just as its predecessor had once stood for the new order of things. As it is, it hides such light as it possesses away from gaze just as effectively as did Hardwick's Propylaeum.

Happily, the current top heirarchy of the BRB seems to be made of worthier stuff than its predecessors of a generation past. There is more concern that important elements of the past should be protected and that this need not be inconsistent with the modern railway. One is not, of course, suggesting that all future development should be some sort of pastiche creation of the past, even though one might wish that the late Sir John Betjeman's 'friendly bombs' should now be asked to fall on the wretched buildings which have been allowed to obscure the front of the new Euston rather than on Slough(!); but maybe it is not too late to hope that an obviously more responsive BRB – especially now that it is itself ensconced in Euston House of all places – might, one day, look again at Euston and see if it can be turned back into a real 'place'. If that were to happen, perhaps the NRM might be persuaded to let Britannia and George Stephenson go home again!

Above The exterior of the new Euston, January 1988. Twenty five years of its existence have not mellowed the view. Robert Stephenson can scarcely be distinguished in the shadows on the right and hardly occupies a prime position, while Euston House (centre distance) fights for survival amongst the new tower blocks.

Below Left Those who remember Platforms 6 and 7 at old Euston will scarce recognise their modern day successors, though honesty compels one to admit that the whole place is much cleaner and vastly more efficient. The train is an unidentified arrival on 7th January 1988, headed by 25kV Class 85 Bo-Bo locomotive No.85003.

Below Right A present-day view of the lodges on Euston Road – compare with the photo on page 21.

Chapter 3

TRAINS FOR ALL PURPOSES

'This is the age of the Train' was the rather ambitious message proclaimed by the advertising hoardings and TV commercials of the late 1970s and early 1980s. Would that it was, for if so, many of our late 20th Century transport problems might well not be so acute as they are. The true age of the train, sadly, died with old Euston and had been creaking at the joints for half a generation previously. In fact, those whose railway knowledge has only been gained in the last quarter century can have little direct knowledge of just what the 'age of the train' really meant, either historically or conceptually. This is not to imply that the modern train is in some way inferior to its predecessors – in many cases it is quite the opposite – but rather that, compared with the past, we use trains for but a mere fraction of the roles they pioneered. The L&BR was all about trains and it is not until one studies what contemporary society really understood by the word 'train' that one can fully appreciate its profound influence on the development of our land.

When the L&BR was built, much of that which we currently take for granted in the transport field was still in the future. The demand was there – or else why build the railway at all – and the nature of the traffic could, to some extent, be predicted, but what could not be foreseen was the quantum rate at which growth was to take place and the incredible ramifications to which it would lead. Not surprisingly, the early trunk railways had to bear the brunt of this 'learning curve' of experience and it was only later – and then not always in Britain – that subsequent railways could take advantage of the experience gained by the pioneers. In many ways, the trains themselves formed almost a 'mobile replay' of the mistakes of Euston.

However, at this point, a caveat should be entered. So far, the L&BR has been treated more or less in isolation but in terms of trains (or, indeed, locomotives for that matter – see Chapter 4), the requirements of the much larger system of which it soon became part were much more significant than those of the purely London and Birmingham part *per se*. Indeed, so rapid was the evolution of railway vehicles during the first ten years after its opening that only two years after the formation of the LNWR, a contemporary writer could state:

"It will not be denied by anyone who has watched the progress of the various companies consolidated under the title of the London & North Western since their formation, that the character of their moving plant has greatly improved. The plain, confined, and somewhat rude passenger carriages have become capacious, elegant, and easy.

The waggons, originally adapted for 3½ tons, have given way before a gradual infusion of stock equal to six tons load, with corresponding strength of build; and the small 12-inch cylinder engines, which with difficulty drew a light mail train at 22½ miles an hour (the London & Birmingham contract speed in 1840), have been superseded by powerful locomotives, maintaining an average speed of 40 miles an hour with heavy trains." (quoted in the *Railway Gazette*, September 1938).

The present writer cannot find it in himself entirely to endorse the 'capacious, elegant, and easy' description of contemporary carriages (sic!), but that there was rapid progress there can be no real doubt. Moreover, though sometimes encountering periods of stagnation, the process of improvement has been continuous since that time, even though some of it, in the early days, was conducted against a background which was not without hostility. The same source quoted above also relates that, in 1845, the railway was perceived by some as:

"a fearful and wide-spreading evil which has broken forth amongst the people of this country, and which threatens to uproot the foundations of society and to poison the fountains of morality and virtue."

. . . or alternatively:

"The farmer is told that the railroad will open a way for a more speedy and profitable disposal of his produce at distant markets, though the only practical experience he has of its benefit is the occasional decapitation of a cow or a sheep."

Needless to say, neither of these prophecies of doom turned out to be true – they were, in fact, already looking more than a little foolish at the time they were written – and for the next half century or more, the railways were mostly perceived as being the almost wholly beneficial influence which in fact they usually turned out to be. And this was the important point. It was more the perception of the railway and what it could do than the nature of its actual hardware which helped attract the necessary support and capital to allow the idea to spread so rapidly beyond the mere confines of the L&BR; but even so, there had to be a pioneer!

The L&BR and its associated GJR were not the only pioneers in terms of their influence on vehicle design and train operating, but being partners in the first trunk route out of London, and having the magical 'Stephenson' connection, it was not unnatural that the way by which they set about doing things was viewed with some interest by contemporary engineers and railway planners.

Much of this contemporary interest concentrated, of course, on describing the actual operational hardware of the newly developing railways, particularly in the realm of locomotives and rolling stock. Traditionally, of course, this aspect of the railway has always been given a sort of literary primacy and is not entirely omitted in this account. However, since so much detailed literature is already available in this field, it seems more useful to look at the overall subject of train travel as it evolved down the years, trying to identify those areas where the L&BR and its successors may have played some significant part in the more widespread development of the basic fundamentals.

We start our more detailed look at the task with what was, for many years, the 'bread and butter' trade of the railway – goods traffic (or freight as it was increasingly to be called as the years went by). The railway idea had evolved from the need for this kind of traffic and the L&BR was no exception. In this case, however, just as with the somewhat earlier L&MR but on a much larger scale, the whole concept of goods traffic was to undergo a fundamental re-appraisal.

Early horse-drawn railways had been concerned, for the most part, with bulk haulage of a single commodity (usually coal, limestone or some other mineral product) and their concern was mainly to provide an expeditious way of getting this material from its source to a suitable transfer point for more convenient onward movement. This was usually by water – canals and rivers in the case of inland sources and often by sea in the case of near-coastal locations. By its very nature, the traffic was mostly one-way and empty vehicles usually had to be returned in this condition to the loading point before they could resume earning any more revenue. There was little, if any need or opportunity for a 'return load' – and the distances involved were frequently too short for it to matter too much anyway.

These line drawings, reproduced from the book 'Railway Machinery' by D.K. Clark, published in the early 1850s, show something of the character and variety of early LNWR goods stock which helped set the pattern for much of Britain. They show a cattle wagon, open and closed goods wagons, low sided and timber wagons, a coke wagon and the all-essential brake van. Their descendants held sway for almost a century.

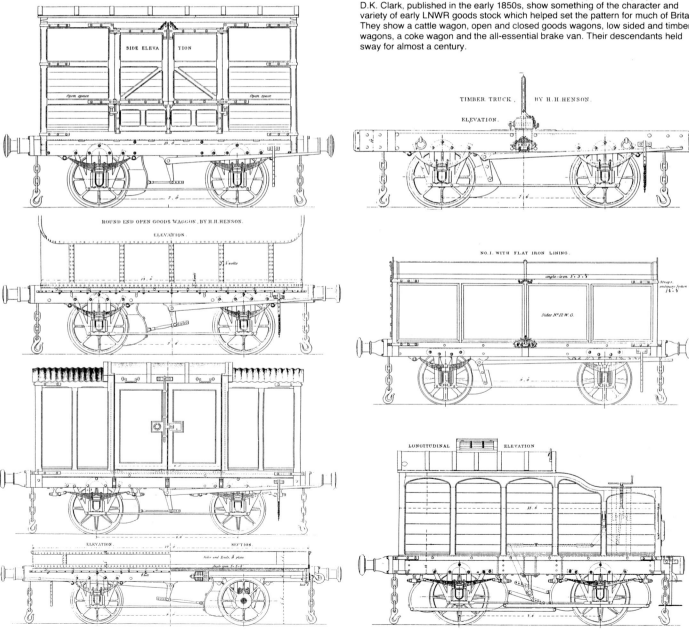

The new steam railway did not alter the nature of this sort of traffic but it did offer opportunity to convey a much higher proportion 'all the way to the consumer' rather than waste time and effort in transfer facilities. It was also much quicker and gave real competition to the waterways, all of which had the immediate effect of cheapening the price of the commodity itself, particularly coal, and it was not long before cavalcades of coal for London began to work their way down the L&BR to the waiting markets, as indeed they did down many another of the main lines as they too were built towards London. It allowed energy for industry and warmth for the domestic hearth to be just as readily provided in London as anywhere else and was undoubtedly a prime factor in the London region growing to be the largest single industrial concentration in Britain without the benefit of indigenous mineral deposits. Coal haulage to the Metropolis has been a railway staple ever since.

Of course, this did not get rid of the 'returned empties' problem – nor does it even today – but such is the advantage of the railway for this kind of business that it has always been able to compete. But there was a new sort of traffic on offer in the early days of the mechanised railway which its horse-drawn predecessor had not really addressed or even identified as being suitable for rail. This was the 'general merchandise' category and the speedy growth of its movement round the country by rail was to sow the seeds of most features of the modern distribution trade.

The origins are hard to identify with precision, but the need probably went back to the dawn of modern industry in the 18th Century. Put at its most fundamental, there was little point in expanding factory output (regardless of end product) if raw material could not be moved to the factory or if the end product itself could not be sold; this also implied movement, this time to the markets. This is so obvious that it seems hardly worth mentioning at all, yet the writer, by virtue of his job, is so regularly surprised at how little real perception of the distribution needs of industry is held by modern society, that a short diversion seems to be in order.

If you were to ask the modern child (or many an adult for that matter!) how the goods which he or she purchases got into the high street shop from which they were bought, the chances are that one would be greeted with a degree of surprised bafflement. Whether this be born of genuine ignorance or is merely a manifestation of astonishment that such a question should be asked is largely irrelevant. The fact is that the late 20th Century citizen assumes that consumer goods (however defined) will somehow be made available by means of local distribution outlets and is very surprised (or angry!) when this does not happen. He or she would, perhaps, be even more surprised to discover that things were not always so. If

Serving London has always been a prime freight role of the L&BR and this 1935 view at Bourne End typifies the LMS approach to the task. It shows a northbound train of coal empties, most of which are the special high capacity bogie wagons built by the LMS to meet the needs of the Stonebridge Park power station. The train engine is LMS Class 4F 0–6–0 No.4150. Note the fine array of LNWR signals and the immaculately manicured track.

Merchandise too was a staple traffic of the line. This is a fully brake-fitted train of vans in the London suburbs early in the century headed by LNWR 'Experiment' Class 4–6–0 No.291 *Leander*.

then pressed to hazard a guess as to when it became so, the modern day consumer is likely to be equally uncertain, which is, of course, a back-handed compliment to the distributors. And it is a fair certainty that many would never appreciate that it was the railway which developed the process to the degree we expect and with which we are familiar today.

Prior to the mechanised railway, only the very well-to-do could, for the most part, afford those products manufactured or originating at any distance from their point of sale, largely because, relative to absolute commodity value, transport costs loomed so high. Small wonder therefore that industrialists and businessmen of the North and Midlands looked with envy at the London market (already approaching 2,000,000 even in the 1830s) and were only too willing to subscribe, often handsomely, to any new form of transport which might enable them to sell their wares more abundantly. This, of course, was nothing new. Josiah Wedgwood, for example, that famous potter of the 18th Century, had done much to promote canal growth to enable him not only to bring his essential China Clay from Cornwall to the Potteries (via coastal shipping and the Trent and Mersey Canal) but also to export his finished product; but the railways added a whole new dimension to this sort of established idea.

If truth be told, the Liverpool and Manchester Railway was a first reaction to and a first revelation of the potential of this new kind of goods traffic but the L&BR (and its imitators) took it into new and hitherto unexploited fields. For one thing, the scope was greater, both in terms of the broader geographical extent of the railway itself and the consequential increased variety of product available; secondly, the demands of the industrial regions, particularly the London market,

pretty well guaranteed success if only the stuff could be got there and thirdly, unlike the mineral trade, there was a fair prospect of a return revenue load of goods flowing the other way. Thus, for example, our above quoted farmer could quite readily accept the (hypothetical?) risk of a decapitated sheep or two when offset against the near certainty of the captive London market and a good price for his surplus produce. This would then, perhaps, allow him sufficient profit to be able to purchase other items (from that self-same market) which the railways were only too happy to bring back to him on another of their goods trains! And there were hundreds and thousands of people who saw it just this way. How, then, did the railway tackle this new and potentially lucrative source of revenue?

It took form in two ways. Firstly, of course, was the actual provision of vehicles to handle the commodities and secondly were the associated facilities for loading, unloading and distribution – the 'Goods Yards' as they were soon to become known. Between them they revolutionised merchandise handling. We start with the vehicles.

The humble four-wheel goods wagon, now almost a thing of the past, drew its shape and character from its mineral-carrying forebear. It was nothing much more than an open wooden (occasionally metal) box on wheels, whose original size must have been related to that which, when fully laden, a good strong horse could pull with no great difficulty. That a steam locomotive could cope with a much larger vehicle seems not, at first, to have been exploited to any great extent and the first steam-hauled goods vehicles were very much in the 3–4 ton haulage range of the railway horse; they simply moved more of them at a time with the steam locomotives. In a curious sort of way, this size proved quite beneficial for decades since, within the goods yards, horses could continue to be used – and were – for moving the four-wheelers about.

In time, more specialised variants (sometimes with roofs and, if so, most usually called vans) began to make an appearance for some of the more vulnerable and/or valuable cargoes, but roofed or not, the traditional four-wheeler held sway. It had very simple springing and coupling, and very primitive hand brakes, if indeed the latter were present at all, and it multiplied at an astonishing rate – clearly indicative of the pent-up demand for the service it could offer.

That the horse still had an important role to play well into the more modern era is well exemplified by this view of the weighbridge at Camden Goods in the later 1930s. Motor traffic is in evidence but the horse still reigns supreme. Of particular interest is the loaded container on the two horse dray next in line for the weighbridge; 'Freightliners' are nothing new!

This charming pair of contemporary LNWR publicity views shows horse-drawn goods in transit by road for transshipment to rail at Camden and Broad Street respectively. The latter location was, of course, on the North London line but one can wager those hops were bound for a brewery somewhere on the LNWR main line via the connection at Chalk Farm!

In due course, as already stated, the weight of goods wagons and their carrying capacity increased somewhat, but save for a few noteworthy specialised exceptions, even at the

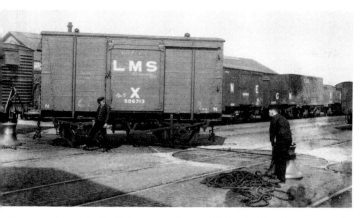

The constraints of the fixed infrastructure imposed during the Victorian era are well illustrated by this mid-1930s view of a quite modern automatically braked LMS van whose modest size only just fits onto the old-fashioned wagon turntable; yet it was just about as big as most yards could handle with their primitive rope and capstan methods.

end of the Victorian period (and in far too many cases much later), the basic four-wheel goods wagon betrayed its ancestry, and its size rarely exceeded some 20ft long over buffers to the very end. What is more, right to the end of the steam age, thousands of them ran their lives without any form of automatic brake operable from the locomotive. This was to be their undoing particularly in the face of motorised competition and, although this book is not intended to be a treatise on rolling stock evolution as such, the matter of goods vehicle design does merit some slight further attention. It was, after all, one of the strangest of all ironies that the very traffic which the railways helped to make possible should so often have fallen victim to a competitor largely through the inadequacies of the railway vehicle rather than the railway itself.

The reasons are complex and probably go back to the incredibly rapid expansion during the early days of the L&BR and its imitators. Perusal of contemporary drawings, some of which are offered in this book, will reveal that as early as the 1840s and 1850s the railways had already established (albeit within quite small dimensional parameters) virtually all the vehicle types needed for most of the potential traffic on offer. They were so successful that very soon a degree of conceptual complacency crept in, some of it undoubtedly influenced by the nature of the fixed infrastructure which had grown in their wake (below), but helped by lack of effective competition.

From the 1840s to the end of the Edwardian period (and often much later for that matter), the unbraked, loose-coupled 'goods' train could hold its own against all-comers in spite of its technologically primitive nature. As long as the horse was the fastest road or canal alternative, even a 10–20 mph goods train had the edge, and the railway proprietors (commercial animals almost to a man) could doubtless see no good reason why things should be changed. It would only cost money, whether it be for better or more sophisticated vehicles or more elaborate terminal facilities, and since the railways enjoyed an almost total monopoly – save between themselves as private companies and even then reduced to a considerable extent by a multiplicity of 'agreed' or Government-imposed practices – there was no great incentive for change.

The two world wars changed all this. The first of these conflicts saw the railways strained to capacity in their magnificently successful efforts to move ever-increasing quantities of men and material, carried out under the control of a pseudo-nationalised supreme authority, the Railway Executive Committee. After the war, the railways reverted to their traditional private role – albeit made slightly different by the consequences of the 1923 grouping wherein all the many companies were amalgamated into four big new systems – but there was now a new factor at work – the mechanised goods road vehicle.

Although this type of vehicle had appeared in Edwardian days, the impetus to its rapid development was accelerated by the needs of the military during the war; and after 1918, many ex-servicemen who had been taught by the army to maintain and drive such vehicles took the opportunity of acquiring war-surplus examples at knock-down prices so as to start up new haulage businesses. The moment something faster than a horse and cart could collect and deliver down our highways and byways, the writing was on the wall for some aspects of traditional railway freight operation. To be fair, the new LMS, which had inherited the L&BR from the LNWR in 1923, made a far better fist of meeting this new threat than did some. Even by the time of the grouping, some of its constituents had gone into the mechanised local haulage business with some vigour and the LMS alone accounted for some two thirds of all railway-owned motorised goods vehicles in 1923; but it was 65% of only some 2,000 in total and it was nowhere near enough to hold the fort.

The 1920s and 1930s saw a gradual erosion of the more marginal short-haul freight activity in favour of road haulage all the way and the railways actually did some of it themselves, so things were not, at first, too desperate. In fact, the railways came up with quite a number of ingenious 'total package, door-to-door' operations and if, at this stage, investment capital had been rather more forthcoming, then the LMS and its competitor companies might well have been able to lay down a rather more modern freight handling infrastructure than, in the event, they were able to do. As it was, however, hardly had the real nature of the threat become apparent than the second great conflict intervened, petrol became rationed and the steam railway, for all its faults, was once more called upon to mount a transport rescue act in the national interest, again under unified central control.

It did so – and that right nobly – to an extent far exceeding even that of the 1914–18 war, but the late 1940s saw a virtual replay of the 1920s, save only for the inevitable railway Nationalisation of 1948, as much an economic necessity as a political gesture of faith by the then Labour Government. The railways had moved prodigious quantities of material during 1939–45 with what was, even then, mostly an obsolescent if not obsolete fleet of goods vehicles, scarce differentiated in type from those of the pioneer L&BR. They generated huge extra revenues but the railways were not allowed to keep them. The extra was kept by the Government during the war and never ploughed back afterwards in the form of the new railway investment which was already overdue in 1939.

In consequence, the new 'British Railways' inherited a wonderfully comprehensive network of routes most of whose all-essential freight services were handled largely by vehicles, many of which would not have surprised Robert Stephenson in their technology and whose handling facilities were almost equally byzantine! And before going on to consider what has happened since, this seems the appropriate point at which to examine in more depth the second key aspect of freight haulage, that of the terminal and distribution facilities.

Such was the pent-up demand in the 1830s and 1840s for easier movement of commercial traffic that no sooner had the lines been laid out than almost every settlement of any size began to develop its own railway goods stations. These were usually positioned alongside the passenger facilities and must have been mightily needed for they appeared at a prodigiously fast rate – and in that lay their ultimate undoing. For the most part, their facilities were geared very closely to the physical dimensions of the then prevailing goods wagons without too much thought given to future development potential, and they were made *very* permanent in most cases.

In consequence, the typical goods yards, especially their permanent unloading sheds and warehouses, were designed round the mid-Victorian 'wagon-module', whether it be in terms of cranage, platform unloading facilities, wagon turntables or what have you. By the time that the railways could, quite easily, have produced more efficient, fast moving and above all larger vehicles, it was often too late. In particular, there was great resistance to increasing wagon size since it would involve much rebuilding of permanent handling facilities. Furthermore, because the railways enjoyed such a near-monopoly, there was little contemporary perception (at least not in Victorian days) that the system might ultimately be doomed to failure because of its technically backward nature. But how could they have known? Provided it did not foul the

fixed structures of the line (bridges, tunnels &c) and could be loaded on a goods wagon, virtually anything could be and mostly was moved by the railway. Moreover, while ever horses and carts (the latter in ever-increasing size, complexity and variety to suit ever more specialised cargoes) could make the essential linkage between the railway goods station and the point of origin/destination of the consignment, God was probably felt to be 'still in his heaven and all right with the world.'!

At first, the motor vehicle began to replace the horse and cart in the purely local sense – the famous 'mechanical horses' of the 1930s at once spring to mind – but the horse and cart 'local' delivery service clung on doggedly. In 1937, the LMS still had five times more horse-drawn commercial vehicles than motorised equivalents (16,344 and 3,270 to be exact) and most of them were to be found at the very heart of the freight handling system, at places like Camden Goods, Curzon Street and so forth. Yet, and in spite of the fact that this was also the year of the ultra-modern, streamlined 'Coronation Scot' passenger trains, there still does not seem to have been too much serious awareness of or apprehension about the implications of the possible road threat. One hesitates to call it complacency – the inter-war railways were

Inherited difficulties notwithstanding, the railways, even before the 1923 grouping, showed themselves well able to tackle most freight loads which would fit the structure gauge of the system. These LNWR views show a special low-centre trolley wagon constructed for outsize loads (here seen conveying locomotive boilers) and two views at Camden Goods: an eight-horse team seen tackling the road-rail interchange of a substantial steel girder load and a consignment of Argyll taxis for London being driven off Caledonian Railway Motor Car Vans of the type shown on the left of picture. 'Motorail' too has rather ancient origins!

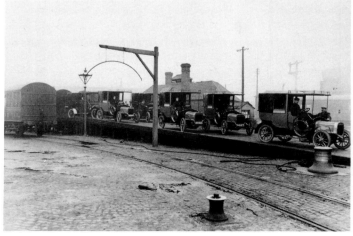

anything but that — but, in retrospect, it seems very much akin to the equally slow growth of awareness of the potential of the railway itself a century earlier.

Of course, while ever the motorised road vehicle could carry no more than a typical railway goods wagon, nor proceed at more than the statutory 20 mph, it doubtless seemed less of a threat, but just as the 1914–8 war had speeded up the development of the modestly sized vehicle, so too did the second global conflagration bring forward the day of the heavier long-distance mechanised road vehicle. If anything, the railways were, in the 1950s, even less prepared for the consequences of this development than they had been for its predecessor in the 1920s.

Even against the most optimistic scenario, it is hard to see the railway ever capturing back the huge variety of freight traffic it once carried or ever again becoming the dominant and near-exclusive haulier it once used to be. No matter how pro-rail one might be, it would not make much sense, nor is

The L&BR was quick to learn from this experience and, from the outset, the likely demands of the passenger were always given considerable attention. This remained the case throughout the subsequent 150 years and it is, of course, as a passenger artery that the route is best known today — and likely to remain so, even if its freight potential does improve. Indeed, the basic alignment of the route was so good in the first place that even were it to be planned today as a modern high-speed and purely passenger railway, it is hard to see how it could be much improved.

Along with the almost contemporary GWR, the L&BR was the first railway which needed to pay attention to the demands of the long distance traveller and it was not too long before the railway began to realise that, unlike the items of cargo in a goods train, a passenger could voice his views as to the nature and quality of the service(s) offered. In due time, he was by no means slow to do so — and has continued in much the same vein ever since (!), an interesting consequence of

Southbound freight 'under the wires' at Bletchley in 1968, headed by 25kV Class AL6 Bo-Bo No.E3186, now Class 86 No.86025. One of the less happy consequences of the pioneering nature of the 25kV electrification on the L&BR was the massively heavy (and ugly) nature of the 'overhead', mercifully not repeated in most of the more modern conversions to ac electric traction.

the present railway infrastructure capable of resuming all its former roles. But while ever railways continue to haul freight and particularly if they manage to regain a significant proportion of the traffic which should, perhaps, never have left them in the first place, it is hard to conceive this happening without the L&BR again playing a major part, a role it has never really lost in the passenger transport field, the area to which we must now turn.

Passenger carrying railways are almost, but not exactly, contemporaneous with the fully mechanised railway itself. With the exception of a few maverick and arguably untypical horse-drawn operations between 1807 and the opening of the Liverpool and Manchester line in 1830, the latter event was the true beginning of modern passenger transport. In fact, the strength of demand for passenger travel took the original proprietors by surprise. They had expected that their line would be of prime use in solving freight haulage problems in South Lancashire and, in due course, this is exactly what happened, but although they had also made provision for passenger travel, it undoubtedly came as something of a revelation when they discovered that for a fair number of years after opening, passenger revenue was greater than that from goods traffic.

which has been that the evolution of passenger carriages, after a somewhat unenterprising start, was soon to be as rapid as that of the goods vehicles was slow. Most of this evolution was in response to the increasing demands and expectations of the paying customer and much of it was to lay firm foundations for all which we now regard as the 'norm' in terms of public transport, no matter whether it be rail, road or air.

In the pioneering days, the L&BR and its 1846 successor, the LNWR, were neither better nor worse than any other railways of the time and placed great reliance on the basic three-compartment carriage configuration established by the L&MR as early as 1830. This idea simply mounted what were, in effect, three stage coach bodies (without, of course, their roof mounted seats, save for the guard) on a single four-wheel chassis and strung them together in 'trains' to meet whatever demand was present. The first class was the best (equivalent to the old 'inside' seats on a stage coach) and the second class, basically designed to offer a solution for the sort of traveller who had, hitherto, ridden on top of the stage coach, was a sort of poor relation alternative with bare boards in place of upholstery, but otherwise built in much the same way. The third class was dreadful. Starting life as a basic open-topped box (in fact some of the earliest second class carriages had also

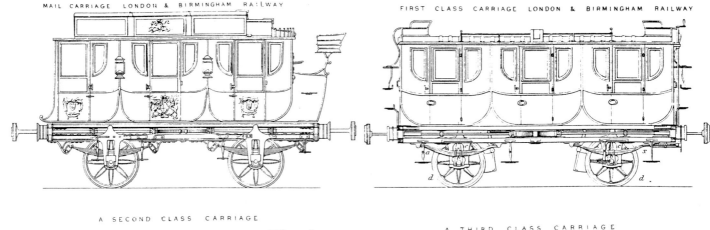

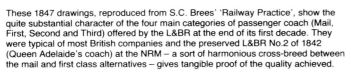

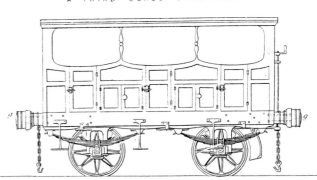

These 1847 drawings, reproduced from S.C. Brees' 'Railway Practice', show the quite substantial character of the four main categories of passenger coach (Mail, First, Second and Third) offered by the L&BR at the end of its first decade. They were typical of most British companies and the preserved L&BR No.2 of 1842 (Queen Adelaide's coach) at the NRM – a sort of harmonious cross-breed between the mail and first class alternatives – gives tangible proof of the quality achieved.

been open-topped) the third class carriage, often without even seats, offered basic accommodation to those who had hitherto, if they travelled at all, paid a modest pittance to ride with the goods on a horse-drawn road wagon at maybe 1–2 mph at best! Although Gladstone's 1844 Act forced the often reluctant railways to roof over these primitive horrors and put them on at least one train per day (the so-called and often best-forgotten 'Parliamentary' trains), third class travel was by no means the amenable form of travel which it eventually became.

For some 40 years or so after the opening of the L&B railway, carriage development was abysmally slow. In part this was due to the fact that the newly developing railways did not have to try too hard and the L&BR/LNWR was no exception. Speed of transit and much cheaper fares were far better than anything the stage coaches could offer hitherto and there is no doubt that, without any really effective competition, complacency set in. The LNWR was a proud but frugal company. It believed in service but also in paying dividends, and its senior officers were not willing to invest if they could see no need. They had what amounted to a captive market and although the customers might complain – there is, in fact, not much evidence that they did except in the realm of catering – they had nowhere else to go. Thus, not until other rival companies began to offer something better in the way of creature comforts, on competing routes between the same centres as those served by the LNWR, did the oldest trunk line of them all begin to pay the matter serious attention; and

it has to be stated that the specific London–Birmingham requirement was not the prime cause. The improvements which eventually happened were, in fact, far more a result of the much wider field of action of the, by now, giant LNWR system.

The catalyst was the Midland Railway, based on Derby, whose rivalry with the LNWR has already been touched upon. In the 1870s, the MR abolished second class, put third class carriages onto *all* trains (this was revolutionary at the time since no company was obliged so to do); it then compounded the gesture by giving third class passengers second class standards of comfort at no extra charge and, to cap all, finally proceeded to reduce first class fares to second class levels. This (seeming) generosity was, of course, wrapped up in a fair amount of contemporary and at times rather sanctimonious grandiloquence regarding offering better travelling conditions to the public but in fact it was mainly a hard-nosed commercial challenge to its competitors and it worked!

The LNWR did not like it – neither, for that matter did most of the other railways with whom the MR was in competition – but whereas some of the others tended to let matters slide, the LNWR was made of sterner stuff. It took a little time to 'get its act together', to use a modern expression, but when it eventually did so, it leapt to the forefront of long distance passenger travel amenity in terms of vehicle design and provisioning, a position which, allowing for the exceptions consequent upon making such a generalisation, it and its successors never really lost for more than half a century; they were certainly instrumental in establishing most of the basic elements of currently accepted standards and some would aver that, contemporary design fashions excepted, they have never been bettered.

Above Queen Adelaide's carriage is the sole surviving passenger vehicle from the L&BR but it could not be a finer specimen: probably the most outstanding 'first generation' four-wheeler in genuinely original condition anywhere in the world. It is seen here inside the Royal Train shed at Wolverton in 1956, alongside King Edward VII's saloon, the latter still in LMS livery. The interior view shows the 'bed' compartment made up for night use.

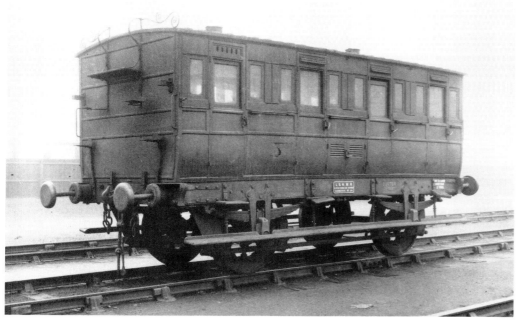

Carriage evolution was slow in early Victorian days, but the carriages were well built. This second generation LNWR four-wheeler was still in use in LMS departmental service in the early 1920s. Apart from the extra compartment (there were usually three in very early carriages), nothing of real significance has changed.

Even towards the end of the nineteenth century, LNWR carriages were not particularly renowned for their elegance – that distinction was to come later. This charming period view, reproduced from an old LNWR postcard, shows two motley collections of mostly four and six wheel stock at Bushey Troughs. There may be a few later carriages in the express on the left: it is rather hard to be certain.

The pioneer 'Corridor' of 1893 – a 'posed' picture of one of the sets of 42ft corridor coaches (plus no fewer than three dining cars) for the principal Anglo-Scottish workings headed by Webb's Famous compound 2–2–2–0 loco No.1304 *Jeanie Deans*.

Such a statement demands qualification and the present writer has already attempted to do so elsewhere[1]. He may therefore, quite understandably, be accused of prejudice; but let us consider the facts. Even as early as 1869, and long before the MR challenge, the LNWR had already built the first gangwayed carriages in Britain – they were, in fact, the favourite conveyances for the reigning monarch – and in 1893, the first proper 'corridor' train was offered to the ordinary passenger between Euston and Scotland. Between 1895 and 1905, the LNWR built more magnificent sleeping and dining cars than any two other companies added together and in 1907–8 delivered the most magnificent set of vehicles ever offered to the non-supplementary fare passenger between London and Scotland. This was no bad record and the LMS, in

Edwardian Elegance: the magnificent set of 12-wheelers, mostly built for use on the 1908 '2 pm' train, are seen here heading north through the outer London suburbs before the First World War behind an unidentified 'George the Fifth' Class 4-4-0.

[1]'An Illustrated History of LNWR Coaches'

succession, continued the good work, so let us examine how this came to be.

By the later years of Victoria's reign, it was beginning to become quite apparent that the traveller had developed quite sophisticated requirements by comparison with those prevalent at the start of the railway age. There was no real competition, save for rival railway companies, yet the major concerns felt in some way obliged to take note and, in consequence, began to produce some of the most gracious, elegant and well thought out conveyances ever offered to the general public. It would have been surprising had not the LNWR played a major part in this development – in fact, the more surprising fact is that it took so long to 'join in the game' so to speak – but when it finally elected to take part, its contribution was immensely significant. The instrument of this change was Wolverton Works, a place first chosen by

Robert Stephenson as the central depot for the L&BR when he set out the line.

The reason for the selection of Wolverton has already been covered and the place is, these days, perhaps most famous as the home of all that is really significant about royal railway travel in Britain. As such, it will always have its place in railway history, but its story goes back long before its regal association. It is, if you like, the father and mother of every 'new town' which has developed in Britain since the 1830s and, in a genuine historic sense, it is by no means inappropriate that the present new city of Milton Keynes should contain within its boundaries such a historic place. It is no mean inheritance.

For quite a number of decades after Wolverton was chosen as the central depot for the fledgling L&BR, it was the main works for the whole of the line, producing both locomotives and coaches. The former must await the next chapter for it was as a major carriage building establishment that Wolverton was, in due course, to become internationally famous. That it did so was almost accidental and bound up mainly with the requirements of the succeeding LNWR.

When the LNWR was formed in 1846, by far the largest elements of the new company were the L&BR and the Grand Junction Railway. Each of them had, by the time of their amalgamation, established considerable works facilities, both on what would now be called 'green field' sites. Wolverton was the senior of the two, having been 'in situ' since the opening of the line itself in 1838, but it would have been a brave man, even in 1846, who would have tried to give second place to the GJR's workshops at Crewe, even though this place did not go into action until 1843. Thus, the new LNWR 'kept the peace' by maintaining both establishments as 'all-embracing' workshops, and replacing the original L&BR and GJR nomenclatures of the two main parts of its system with 'Southern Division' and 'Northern Division' respectively. For many years, this 'status quo ante' was maintained, each place having its own chief. By 1861, these positions were occupied by two very eminent men in the locomotive business: J. Ramsbottom at Crewe and J.E. McConnell at Wolverton. The latter was the more senior, and retired at the end of the year, at which point the LNWR sensibly appointed Ramsbottom as locomotive chief for the whole system. The immediate effect, of course, was that the 'Crewe' approach to locomotive matters became dominant and, hardly to be wondered at, Wolverton built its last new locomotives (to the McConnell pattern) as early as 1862. However, for another 15 years it remained an all-purpose works and was responsible for maintaining both locomotives and rolling stock.

Until 1864, LNWR carriages were built at Saltley (Birmingham) and repaired at several locations, including Euston and Crewe; but in that year, the LNWR resolved to concentrate its carriage building at Wolverton. This naturally caused consequential changes and in 1877, somewhat inevitably one feels, the locomotive department closed and Wolverton became solely concerned with non-locomotive matters. In due course this included the making and repairing of wagons (along with Earlestown in Lancashire), the fabrication of all manner of small items from wheelbarrows to horse drawn carts and, in its later days, the bodywork of road motor vehicles. However its principal claim to fame was always as the exclusive carriage building and repair establishment for the whole of the LNWR, as was Crewe on the locomotive side; for just as Wolverton had lost its locomotive tasks, so too did Crewe abandon its carriage repair shops in 1878. In retrospect, this move to specialisation at both places can now be seen to have worked to the mutual benefit of each of them, for they both became justly famous. In the case of Crewe this was a fairly instant matter – for its affairs were now in the charge of the immortal F.W. Webb – but as far as Wolverton was concerned, it was a decade or more before the world began to sit up and take note of what was happening there. Before considering this, however, we must first take a brief look at the 'geography' of this famous place.

The original works were set up on the west (or down) side of the original passenger station built at this approximately half-way point between London and Birmingham. Although the

Some of the less well-known products of the old L&BR works at Wolverton are featured in these four views viz: LMS rug and pillow barrow for use in connection with night time travel, LMS 12cwt horse-drawn parcel van, Wolverton-bodied LNWR 4-ton AEC road motor for the conveyance of 'demountable flats' (this example based at Coventry) and the very stylish 1932 Wolverton parcel van bodywork on a Ford chassis. In all cases, the attention to livery and finish is outstanding.

bulk of the expansion – which was rapid – took place at right angles to the main line along the north side of the road leading west to Stony Stratford, expansion also took place on the east side which had the undesirable effect of leaving the original main line cutting through the middle of a 'split' works site. Curiously enough much the same also happened at Crewe and the solution adopted at both places was rather similar – a new deviation line. By the mid-1870s, the need was obvious for quadrupling the main line anyway, so at Wolverton, this need was combined with solving the works problem and four new deviation tracks were built to the east of the whole complex. The engineering work was enormous – amongst other things it included the widening of the original Wolverton viaduct

The 'new' Wolverton station after the alterations of 1878–82 was approached from the bridge-located booking office on the Stony Statford–Newport Pagnell road. It still is, but the Wolverton to Stony Stratford tramway seen here steam-hauled c.1900 is no more.

not to mention several new bridges and a totally new station – and took nearly as long as building the whole of the L&BR in the first place. It started in 1878 and by 1882 the new Wolverton station, the present one in fact, was completed and open for traffic.

The old main line now became a purely internal line within the works and is still there to this day. It is no longer surrounded by active shops – those still in use are all alongside the road at Stony Stratford – but the old line will probably continue to be the point of entry to Wolverton Works from the main line while ever railway vehicles are repaired there.

It was some time after carriage building and repair was concentrated at Wolverton that its fame began to develop and this was probably due to two main factors: the nature of the LNWR heirarchy in general and the character of the carriage chief himself, one Richard Bore. On the company side, the LNWR had some formidable men at the helm. One of these was its chairman, Richard Moon, and he was more than ably abetted by his chief engineer, Francis William Webb who, though based at Crewe in charge of locomotives, also determined the essential mechanical engineering policy at Wolverton in terms of carriage running gear. Neither of them could see much point in spending more than they needed and this was as true of carriages as anything else.

Bearing in mind its prime trunk route status, the LNWR had nothing much to boast about in mid-Victorian days as far as carriages were concerned. It was no worse than most of the others but was by no means innovative and, in respect of carriage brakes, it bordered on the disgraceful. This was largely because of Webb's insistence for many years on the use of the Clark and Webb chain brake, a primitive contraption of no great efficiency which he had helped patent and for whose efficacy he had a much higher regard than almost anyone else! Moreover, Webb also preferred to use his own sideways-moving 'radial' axles at the end of longer vehicles to help them traverse curves. These were not too bad with six-wheelers but bordered on the ridiculous when adopted for eight-wheelers rather than the much more sensible pivoting bogie.

Richard Bore seems to have been a compliant accomplice in all this sorry business. He came to Wolverton from the old carriage works at Saltley in 1864 and never seems to have asserted himself at all. He was, sad to say, a rather unimaginative carriage designer even by the standards of the day and did little at all to improve the general quality of most LNWR

The majority of Webb's 'radial' axle carriages were probably those with eight wheels, but he also assayed the idea in an attempt to extend the length of six-wheelers. This view shows 32ft 6in long six-wheel invalid saloon No.28 thus equipped, the fixed axles being the two nearer the camera; the movable radial truck is at the far end of the vehicle. The general vehicle styling is wholly typical of 19th Century LNWR practice.

Queen Victoria's Royal Train in the pre-1895 period was mostly formed from a motley collection of mainly six-wheel carriages plus a few radial eight wheelers. It is seen here behind the Webb 3-cylinder compound 2–2–2–0 No.410 *City of Liverpool* and the Queen's twin saloons feature as vehicles number six and seven in the formation. Rebuilt on a bogie underframe in 1895, the Queen's saloon survives at the National Railway Museum.

carriages, which remained stodgily unchanged until the 1880s. Yet Richard Bore is remembered above all for one quite spectacular piece of carriage building which took place in 1869 – the construction of a new saloon for HM Queen Victoria. More properly, it was two six-wheel vehicles separated by the first ever access gangway to be fitted between a pair of carriages in Britain, and it survives at the National Railway Museum in its rebuilt 1895 form.

From all other standpoints, however, nothing really improved at Wolverton until Bore retired in 1886, to be replaced by a man of altogether different and greater stature, C.A. Park. He was, if you like, the carriage and wagon equivalent of F.W. Webb and was acutely aware how backward LNWR carriage design had become compared with some other railways. However, it took some time for him to make improvements. Webb had already abandoned the chain brake for new carriages in 1881 but it did not vanish until 1892 – and then only because of government legislation compelling the use of automatic continuous brakes on carriages. Park was no more enchanted with the radial underframes than he was with the chain brakes but these too had to wait until 1892 before they were abandoned in favour of bogies. It was probably no coincidence that the autocratic Richard Moon had retired from the chairmanship of the LNWR in 1891!

Setting aside a few, mainly insignificant exceptions, the thrust of the demand for better amenity in the last quarter of the 19th Century was directed towards meeting three main requirements of creature comfort: toilet facilities, sleeping and eating. The provision of lavatories was adopted – admittedly with some reluctance – by most companies, including the LNWR. After all, these things, at times almost unmentionable in the Victorian context, took up extra space and generated no additional revenue! However, they had to be provided and the LNWR, as did others, offered quite a few ingenious solutions to the problem. In the event, although many various and valiant attempts were made to insert the essential lavatories between conventional compartments, the logical solution of the continuous corridor was eventually to be adopted and the LNWR did so with great vigour, certainly more than any other system from the mid-1890s onwards. As such, although not unique, the LNWR, as the major provider of such amenity, set the standards for all. And it did much the same for sleeping and eating facilities.

The early 1890s, therefore, marked the start of a new era at Wolverton. It began with a well-publicised attempt in 1893 to produce new carriages for the West Coast Joint Stock (WCJS). They did not look especially different from their predecessors, save for the dining cars, neither were they very long (only 42ft) but they had bogies and, most important of all, a corridor was provided throughout the length of the whole train. This was only the second 'full train' example of this feature in Britain and for decades afterwards, the service it operated from Euston, the 2pm to Edinburgh and Glasgow, was known as 'The Corridor', even when most trains were corridor-equipped. In LMS days, the same service became known as the 'Mid-Day Scot'.

This 1893 train marked the beginning of a period wherein progress was as rapid as it had previously been slow. By the end of the century, Wolverton was building corridor carriages for the whole of the parent LNWR system, as well as for the WCJS, and their length had risen to 50ft. In terms of basic design they were, perhaps, not greatly different in principle from anyone else's, but Wolverton and the LNWR tended to build rather more of them than most. Even so, had it been left at this point, one doubts whether Wolverton's subsequent reputation would have been greatly different from that of any other carriage building establishment. That it became so can only be explained in the context of its soon to become supreme role in the design and evolution of specialised carriages, particularly dining and sleeping cars.

These areas were a little different, for here there was a real opportunity for additional revenue if some suitable form of conveyance could be contrived. Thus, starting in the late 1870s, both matters were addressed and although the LNWR was the pioneer in neither field, it was undoubtedly to become the leader in both categories by the end of the pre-grouping period. It is a moot point which of the two is more important and, indeed, the present BR administration is faced with a not dissimilar problem.

The demand for meals on trains arose from the fundamental differences between railway travel and that of the preceding stage coach era. In the old days, it was quite reasonable to break journey at a suitable inn (maybe while horses were changed and/or the staff refreshed) to partake of refreshment, so, hardly surprisingly, the railways at first tried to copy this. Thus, at places like Wolverton, there arose refreshment rooms to substitute for the old coaching inns. However, one of the advantages of the new railway was its speed, so any long waits for refreshment were inevitably bound to mitigate against this idea. In consequence, meal breaks were curtailed to such a point that travellers could scarcely partake of the meal for which they had paid in advance (of course!), before the train was ready to depart. In extremis, this could result in customers having paid for the whole meal failing to get past the soup course — and they objected, vociferously in many cases. The result, inevitably, was the 'meals on wheels' concept of the dining car, introduced on the Great Northern Railway in 1879, but taken to its ultimate and quite magnificent conclusion, in the pre-1923 context, by the purpose-built dining cars of the LNWR. Their design, encapsulated forever in such examples as the preserved 1900 example at the National Railway Museum, has never been bettered.

It has been noted how the character of the passenger *train* changed quite remarkably during the last quarter of the 19th Century, led by the Midland Railway; it now remains to be explained why and how Wolverton and the LNWR eventually overtook their rivals in terms of carriage *design*. The original motivation was, of course, inter-company competition but this, on its own, might only have led to the LNWR catching up and then remaining 'on par' with the opposition. In fact, however, it did rather more than this and to explain something of the phenomenon we must first consider the influential part played by another parallel line of passenger carriage development which was taking place in late Victorian Britain, namely the activities of the British Pullman Car Company. Curiously, the Midland Railway was again involved.

George Mortimer Pullman, an American, introduced new and, by contemporary standards, markedly superior Transatlantic ideas of comfort and carriage design into Britain at the invitation of the Midland Railway in 1874. The subsequent story is exceptionally well recorded elsewhere, but in essence, the 19th Century Pullman approach concentrated on greater luxury for the first class passenger, initially in the realm of sleeping cars but ultimately in the provisioning of high quality daytime luxury travel, often accompanied by a complete 'meals at all seats' dining facility, the latter being the functional role by which the word 'Pullman' is still best known on the British railways of the 1980s.

The Midland had a 'blow hot, blow cold' relationship with Pullman and his company, in spite of having introduced the idea to Britain, and this ambivalent attitude largely centred on two issues. The first was the Midland's own, not to mention the general British, dislike of the supplementary charge which Pullman levied for the use of his very fine carriages, or 'Cars' as they were always called. Secondly, as far as the MR was concerned, it probably felt that it could design carriages every bit as good as those of Pullman without a supplementary charge. The MR exercised its 'buy-out' option of the Pullman operating contract in 1888, but continued in a spasmodic way to run Pullman type vehicles under its own name for some time, even buying four new sleeping car bodies from Pullman as late as 1900, which it fitted with its own design of running gear.

Meantime, while other companies (e.g. the London, Brighton and South Coast Railway) espoused Pullman's cause, the LNWR viewed the whole business with some suspicion, not to say a little distaste. During the Richard Moon period, for example, the LNWR would have nothing to do with the technically better vehicle concepts which both Pullman and the MR had pioneered in Britain (larger and stronger carriages with bogies for example) and very little with the design and evolution of more luxurious carriage interiors either. Some few sleeping and dining carriages were built in the 1880s but there was little indication that the LNWR had heard of Pullman, let alone that it could see any virtue in copying his ideas. In fact, however, it rather seems that Mr Park could have been watching matters with rather

The trendsetting 12-wheelers of the 1890s. The shorter of the two is one of the 50ft 6in kitchen/diners, WCJS No.483, for the 1892-3 Anglo-Scottish services while the sleeping car, WCJS No.265, is one of the pioneer 65ft 6in cars which, as early as 1897, established conceptual norms for overnight travel which are still valid in the present day. The distinctively new stylistic linkage is obvious and survived, little changed in essence, until the late 1920s.

more interest than might have been supposed. No sooner had Moon retired from the chair and Park got into his stride, than in 1892–3 (ready for use in the soon-to-be-introduced 1893 corridor trains – above), Wolverton suddenly produced a round dozen of quite spectacularly well-equipped dining cars. They were not very long (they varied between 45ft and 50ft 6in, depending on type) and in some ways were not dissimilar to those which the LNWR had built slightly earlier. But with their massive construction and six-wheel bogies they represented a quantum leap forward in most vital respects and were every bit as good as anything Pullman had made so far and in one respect better – they were for first and third class passengers alike.

In design terms, though some of them kept to the traditional LNWR body styling, most of them displayed an elegant new type of body treatment. They were all given distinctive domed-end clerestory roofs and, on the newer styled vehicles, elaborate entrance lobbies as well, with decorative iron scrollwork supporting the handrails. The Pullman influence was clear but the result was much more quintessentially British and there was *no supplement* for their use. No fewer than three went into each of the new 1893 corridor trains and the public took to them instantly.

This ready acceptance seems to have been all the incentive the LNWR needed to launch itself into a massively comprehensive programme of dining and sleeping car building starting in the mid-1890s. While rival companies like the Midland managed to produce some equally fine vehicles – Wolverton was by no means alone in its craftsmanship – they only did so in small numbers whereas the LNWR eventually ordered them up by the dozen. The length of the dining cars went up to 65ft 6in during 1895 and similarly-styled side

corridor sleeping cars of the now universally accepted interior British layout came in only a year or two later. In both cases, the vehicles were larger, heavier and every bit as well made and technically innovative as those of Pullman or any other company for that matter. It seems fair to deduce that the LNWR's boldness in placing its faith in its own product, while the MR and others were still dithering a little, was instrumental in the more widespread adoption of company-designed sleeping and dining cars by other British railways rather than give Pullman, who had pioneered many of the ideas, a greater opportunity to expand. Certainly by the turn of the century, most of the main line railways had followed Wolverton's rather than Pullman's lead, and Pullman withdrew to something of a 'rump' south of the Thames.

Other companies copied but never improved upon the basic idea (a compact kitchen and pantry combined with passenger seating areas) and the LMS followed suit with some equally splendid examples. The early days of BR could offer no better solution to the problem – there was, in fact, no great need – and even the modern BR dining car, if still offered, is, conceptually, no different from its LNWR or LMS forebear. The LNWR/LMS were not, of course, unique, albeit they were at the forefront, but it is worth reminding readers that, although the modern airline industry has willingly adopted the railway inspired idea of feeding passengers while they travel, it has made no significant improvement upon that which was established a century ago on the oft-maligned railway – even if one gets the best which the first class service on Concorde can offer. The railway was truly the modern trendsetter and has still not been surpassed in terms of sheer quality when called for.

Much the same is also true in terms of night travel. The

The LMS continued in the LNWR tradition with some very splendid 12–wheel dining cars during the 1930s. Here is the smooth-styled and modern exterior of First Class No.27, built at Wolverton in 1933 during the first year or so of the Stanier regime; the stylish interior shows a slightly later example of the same genre, No.37, built at Wolverton in 1936.

ever-extending railway network of Britain fairly quickly gave rise to the need for overnight travel to cover some of the longer distances. Hardly surprisingly, the London and Birmingham section of the LNWR and its descendants, being at the southern end of what ultimately became one of the longest through routes in Britain – that to Inverness and the far north of Scotland – was much involved in this overnight business. Dedicated 'sleeping cars' as such were not to be found in Britain until the 1870s and it was actually a Scottish company, the North British Railway, which introduced the first, for use down the East Coast of the country, but the LNWR was not far behind and by the turn of the century was undoubtedly the British leader in the field, both in terms of quality and numbers of vehicles operated.

The essence of the modern sleeping car evolved during the last decade of Victoria's reign and the LNWR, GWR and East Coast companies were the principal influences. The LNWR needed far more of them and, in consequence, its approach became dominant though all companies which ran such vehicles eventually adopted a similar type – essentially a side corridor carriage with individual single or double berths replacing the conventional compartments. There would, typically, be an attendant's compartment (with a small kitchen/pantry for light refreshments) and maybe a small smoking room as well. The dozen or so people (at most) who could be accommodated in these often palatial vehicles were always first class until 1928. In part this was because dedicated sleeping cars were expensive both to build and operate and thus commanded a supplement for their use. The railways presumably felt that only the first class traveller would be willing or able to meet this cost and for a generation or two this was mostly correct.

Pressure of public demand caused the LMS (along with the GWR and LNER) to extend the facility to third class travellers in 1928, albeit in a somewhat more spartan form, but by the time of nationalisation (it actually started in the later 1930s but was delayed by the second world war), just about the only real difference between a first class and the latest design of third (now second or 'standard') class sleeper was the number of berths in the compartment. A first class compartment had but a single berth, a second class sleeping compartment usually had two, sometimes four. But so similar, in fact, did the facilities eventually become that the latest BR air-conditioned sleeping cars, introduced in the early 1980s, make no class differentiation at all. The second berth is simply left folded out of use if one has paid the first class supplement.

Although slightly less familiar to most people than a day carriage, many folk could and did use sleeping cars simply because there has never been any other form of overnight conveyance (save perhaps a ship's cabin) which can offer quite so much real comfort for those who must travel overnight; certainly the most modern airliner has nothing to rival it. For one thing, quite apart from actually being on the move, one also saves the cost of a hotel room, and many overnight travellers still prefer this to the alternative of trying to sleep in an ordinary seat or getting up in the middle of the night to catch an aeroplane which will arrive at its destination in time for a 9.00am meeting! Thus, the idea has never fallen out of favour and the modern versions are often sought after by such as MPs, commuting from Westminster to their northern and Scottish homes and constituencies at weekends. Moreover, this is one field of travel where the London and Birmingham line will continue to play the prime role, for the BRB has

The pioneering LMS third class sleeping cars of 1928 were not built at Wolverton but they were surely in evidence on the old L&BR section of the West Coast main line. This is No.14247 from the corridor side, little different in style from a conventional carriage, but representing a vast improvement in third class amenity. A preserved sister vehicle survives at the NRM.

recently (1987) stated its intention to concentrate virtually all its London–Scotland overnight services on Euston! They will, of course, make full use of the latest air-conditioned vehicles and, perhaps most surprisingly, the interior layout of these modern vehicles is no whit different in its basic essentials than that established by the LNWR nearly 90 years earlier.

This does not betoken an obsolescent concept; more properly it should be taken as a tribute to the railways for having so early in their evolution come up with fine ideas which stood the test of time. But this sort of forward thinking was not confined to the rather specialised dining and sleeping carriages on which the last few paragraphs have concentrated. The railways have always been at the forefront of passenger vehicle design and it seems appropriate that this chapter should be concluded by taking a brief look at some of the more influential ideas they have pioneered, particularly in the domain of what might be called the 'ordinary' conveyance.

Though the Victorian railways were, for the most part, rather reluctant to provide even a modicum of creature comforts until late in the 19th Century, by the Edwardian period, things were very different. By then, most railways, like the Midland of the 1870s, had either abandoned or were in process of abandoning three class travel. The LNWR itself did it in two stages. The Anglo-Scottish services (operated by 'West Coast Joint Stock', co-owned by the LNWR and the Caledonian, though basically LNWR in design) were first/third only well before the turn of the century and, by 1912, the parent company's domestic services were similarly treated. To be truthful, there had been very little real difference between second and third for a generation before the decision was made to classify them all 'third' and the LNWR came up with some very splendid carriages for the ordinary passenger. Its short-distance suburban and stopping train vehicles were not greatly different from those of most of its rivals but they were better than many and inferior to very few. In all conscience there was little which needed to be changed in this field and their lineal descendants in the form of high density, non-corridor carriages with a side door to each set of seats continued to perform a role, even after electrification, on many lines, including those which led from Euston. They are not quite dead in the late 1980s though Euston sees them no more.

Ordinary carriages on the old LNWR did not show quite such rapid change in style or amenity, but were vital to the economy of the line, none the less. These views show a semi-fast train of non-corridor bogie stock for Broad Street heading south on the 'fast' lines at Bushey and an obviously well-patronised set of six-wheelers on excursion duty at Boxmoor in the Edwardian era.

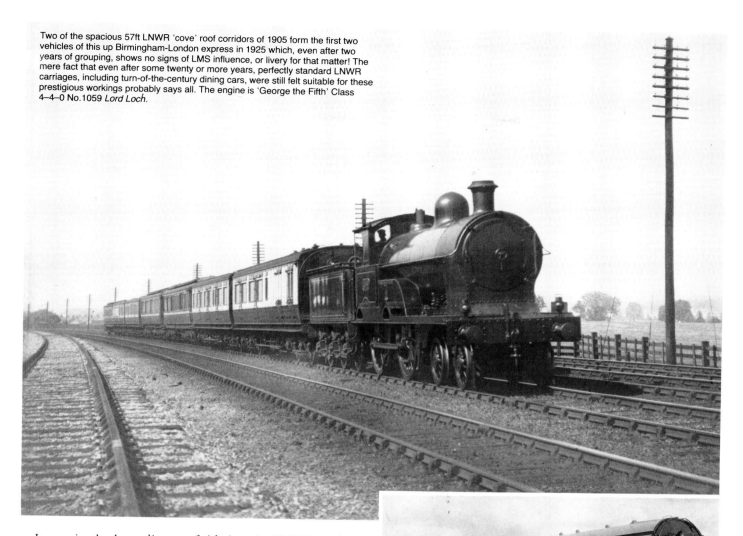

Two of the spacious 57ft LNWR 'cove' roof corridors of 1905 form the first two vehicles of this up Birmingham-London express in 1925 which, even after two years of grouping, shows no signs of LMS influence, or livery for that matter! The mere fact that even after some twenty or more years, perfectly standard LNWR carriages, including turn-of-the-century dining cars, were still felt suitable for these prestigious workings probably says all. The engine is 'George the Fifth' Class 4–4–0 No.1059 *Lord Loch*.

It was in the long-distance field that the LNWR and its LMS successor led the way and nowhere was this more true than in the humble third class corridor coach. As early as 1904–5, the LNWR introduced some magnificent bogie carriages, 57ft long with side corridors, lavatories and only 56 seats even when all were occupied. Only three years later it produced some even more spectacular third class carriages for the Scottish services, this time without the draughty outside doors and with compartments accessible only via a side corridor leading from a palatial end lobby. Other railways copied but never improved on it and by the 1930s the LMS had gone several steps better by giving large 'picture' windows to the third class passenger, along with arm rests and courtesy lights above the seats. Apart from the fact that the compartments themselves were a foot or so smaller between partitions, they held no more passengers than the first class equivalent and even a fully occupied 57ft long third class corridor carriage only seated 42 people! Neither the other rival companies (save in a few rather special cases) nor the BR successor of the 1950s and 1960s ever came up with anything better than the third class vehicles which were accepted as the norm between places such as London and Birmingham – and elsewhere on its parent system – from the early 1930s onwards.

Even where higher seating density was required, the LMS offered, to a far greater extent than any other railway, something rather more amenable than the cramped four per

These LMS corridor composites of the 1930s (exterior view: 1936 series; interior view: third class compartment of 1934) are entirely typical of the high standard of ordinary accommodation which was offered by the descendants of the old L&BR in the final company years.

The move towards 'open' stock was established by the LMS in the 1920s. These pictures show the exterior and interior views of Wolverton-built open brake third No.638 of 1927. Contemporary fashions excepted, they are no whit different in principle from the carriages which form the bulk of present day 'standard class' InterCity day carriages.

side seating of the rival companies' side-corridor third class coaches. It took the form of facing pairs of seats across a table on either side of a central aisle, rather than a side corridor and eventually set the pattern for most succeeding ordinary coaches. Even in the 'high density' mode, it was far more roomy than the growing road coach competitor and today, its lineal descendant in the form of the standard air-conditioned open coach on the various BR InterCity routes, still gives the ordinary traveller far more space than even the most palatial road or air competitor can do.

It would be quite wrong to pretend that all significant steps in this long distance carriage evolution came out of the LNWR and LMS. Many other companies too played their part as did their BR successors, but sheer size would always give the owners of the London and Birmingham line in position of some eminence when it came to innovation. Thus, for example, BR carriage lighting in the first decade or more of nationalisation followed customary LMS practice which itself had been derived from that of the LNWR.

Having raised the subject of interior comfort and amenity, it is also well worth recalling that, quite apart from the toilet, eating and sleeping facilities already discussed, such matters as decent lighting, heating and air conditioning were all applied to ordinary railway carriages long before they became a commonplace in buses, coaches or airliners. Furthermore, one cannot resist the comment that on the one much more recent occasion where design influence went the other way and the railways, during their crisis of self-confidence in the early 1970s, sought to copy the airline industry by recruiting some aircraft specialists to design railway carriages, the result was the Advanced Passenger Train – and we all know what happened to that! That this remark is possibly a little unfair to those genuinely relevant and significant carriage building ideas which came out of this ill-fated project is accepted, but the fact remains that at much the same time, the apparently 'old-fashioned' railway carriage engineers quietly went their

own traditional way and produced the highly successful BR MkIII carriage, now the mainspring of the HSTs, most of the expresses out of Euston (including the above-mentioned and quite splendid sleeping cars), and also the basis of the body construction of much of the new generation of multiple unit stock.

Just as a railway input has always been strong in influencing the general development and perception of public passsenger transport in all modes, the same has also been true of vehicle building itself. The railways at first copied the horse drawn road coaches but soon developed their own ways of doing things which, in due course, fed back again to the mechanised road vehicle and even some early aircraft designs. Body construction, seat design and interior amenity was often a conscious imitation of accepted railway practice and, indeed, in terms of the motor industry in its early days, the technical quality of people trained in the railway engineering industry was put to very good use in the expanding motor trade. The fact that Rolls-Royce set up shop in both Derby and Crewe was no coincidence. And mention of Crewe is no bad cue for introducing the next element of the story – that of the locomotives which pulled the trains.

Chapter 4

KEEPING THE WHEELS TURNING

The L&BR was all about *mechanised* transport and although not literally the first in the field, it was undoubtedly the first global instance where self-propelled machinery was going to move vehicles over such great distance. However, it never stood in isolation; when it opened, *all* locomotive designers were striving to improve their product, often quite rapidly. But it should occasion no surprise that the requirements of the L&BR did play some part in the story. Indeed, there was, in the early days, even a distinctive L&B element to some aspects of locomotive evolution, but this geographical differentiation did not last long. At the same time, however, the requirements of the L&BR line were always germane to the more important developments in railway motive power after 1838 and were, hardly surprisingly, in at the start of some of them. In fact, with a few exceptions, one can trace most of the key elements in the history of British locomotive practice via the machines built firstly for the L&BR and its successors. This will be the object of the next part of our narrative, striving, of course, not to overplay the involvement of the L&BR in the greater story.

It started with the steam locomotive, for the short-lived period of stationary winding engines on Camden Bank ended in 1844 and, in the wider sense, can realistically be ignored. Now by the time the L&BR Act was passed by Parliament, the future form of the steam locomotive had, to all intents and purposes, been set by George and Robert Stephenson with their 'Rocket' locomotive of 1829 for the L&MR. This type evolved rapidly during the next few years and by the mid-1830s, what was to become regarded as the traditional configuration for a steam locomotive had become established.

In simple terms, the basic steam locomotive consisted of a 'water-jacketed' firebox at the rear and a multi-tube boiler in the centre, through whose tubes passed hot gas from the firebox to a smokebox and chimney at the front. Steam, controlled by the driver by means of a 'regulator', was taken through a pipe from the 'steam space' (most commonly achieved by means of a 'dome' projecting above the top of the boiler) to the working parts (cylinders and valve gear) which were normally located below the smokebox with the drive going backwards (with respect to the chimney end) to the driving wheels, by now almost inevitably set to the rear of the cylinders. The exhaust from the cylinders, which gave the characteristic 'puffing' sound to a steam locomotive, was then directed via a blast pipe to the chimney, thus helping to 'draw' the fire through the fire tubes, thus materially assisting combustion of fuel in the firebox itself. This basic idea was

never modified in any fundamental way until the end of steam locomotives themselves and was at the heart of the configuration of 'Planet' and 'Patentee', the first lineal descendants of 'Rocket'; both, needless to say, were designed by Robert Stephenson.

So far so good, but even when the L&BR was built, two or three separate lines of development of this fundamental configuration had already begun to appear, not so much in terms of the basic disposition of the various components, but more in terms of the constructional methods adopted by individual engineers, each of whom was seeking to achieve a more satisfactory end product. Curiously enough, the L&BR at first represented one line of evolution, its ally the GJR another, while the third line was pursued by the near contemporary GWR. It is interesting to note that the eventual successors to the L&BR fell heir to vital elements of all three plus their later developments. It is a fascinating story. Parts of it are semi-technical but overall it does not really require any deep scientific knowledge to appreciate the extent to which railway engineers were pushing to the limits of their then current experience, largely to achieve a more effective product.

The first areas to be considered were those pertaining to the nature of the construction of the locomotive itself. These tended to concentrate on two main areas: the frames of the machine and the disposition of its working parts.

In terms of framing, there were two principal lines of development. The traditional Stephenson approach, exemplified by the pioneering 'Planet' and 'Patentee', eventually favoured the 'flat' or 'plate' frame in which the chassis of the engine was made from flat metal plates (in the earlier days more usually a combination of wood and metal) set vertically to the line of track and to which were then affixed the various components such as wheels, springs, &c. The main early alternative to this approach – and adopted by the L&BR in its first engines – was the use of bar iron to form the frames rather than flat plates. This was very much the forte of the L&BR's first locomotive engineer, Edward Bury. In both the Patentee type and the Bury bar-framed version, the cylinders were set between (or 'inside') the frames below the smokebox and close to the longitudinal centreline of the locomotive. The drive from the cylinders to the wheels was by means of a crank axle.

The third variant arose on the GJR as a result of much breaking of crank axles in the early days. Though often erroneously attributed to Alexander Allan (the GJR works manager who had to cope with the crank axle problem and in

Built in 1835 for the Liverpool and Manchester Railway.
The first engine with inside cylinders.

OLD PASSENGER LOCOMOTIVE
DRIVING WHEELS 5 FT DIAMETER

The 'Bury' style of bar-framed
locomotive could trace its ancestry
back to the Liverpool and Manchester
Railway. This is the first inside-
cylinder example, dating from 1835, of
an original L&MR type soon to
become familiar on the L&BR after
1838.

Below and Opposite The principal
alternative approach in the early days
as far as the L&BR/LNWR were
concerned was the so-called 'Crewe
Type', a robustly constructed outside-
cylindered design, well exemplified
here by 2–2–2 No.1848 *Sefton* of
1848 (for passenger work) and 2–4–0
No.3074 of 1854 (mostly for goods
trains), originally named *Cerberus*,
later *Caliban*. LNWR engine names
were always rather random in their
infinite variety and this characteristic
seems to go back well into history.

fact made a considerable contribution to its solution), the eventually successful design was also very much associated with W.B. Buddicom and Francis Trevithick, originally at Edge Hill, later (after 1843) at Crewe; indeed it is most proper to call it the 'Crewe' type. In this form of locomotive, the typical inner plate frames were combined with cylinders mounted 'outside' them, held secure by a reinforced double frame at the front. The cylinders were connected directly to the outer face of the driving wheel by means of a visible outside connecting rod attached to a crank pin on the wheel.

There was thus no crank axle – a positive virtue – but the much wider apart nature of the cylinders could and did impart a much larger degree of lateral oscillation to the locomotive.

As far as our story is concerned, the pure Patentee was not adopted in any great way by either the GJR or the L&BR. Curiously, however, Brunel on the GWR found it expedient to use Patentee type locomotives in spite of the fact that they were developed by his greatest rival, Robert Stephenson. In fact, throughout the broad gauge era, by far the bulk of the 7ft gauge GWR engines were basically nothing much more than

very large Patentees. Meantime, the two pioneer trunk lines designed by the Stephensons (L&BR and GJR) mostly made use of someone else's development. Interestingly, all three lines of evolution were eventually to lead to a coming together in the 20th Century on the LMS system, but we must start by looking at them separately.

Locomotive affairs on the L&BR were centred upon Wolverton. At first, in 1837, Edward Bury was placed in charge and naturally chose to use his own bar-framed types. His position vis-a-vis the L&BR was slightly unorthodox in that although he was a company employee, the actual engines were purchased by the L&BR from Bury's company in Liverpool (Bury, Curtis and Kennedy) and maintained by that company under contract for the first three years. Bury much favoured the four-wheeler but this imposed size and stability constraints which, as the years went by, became ever more irksome and led to much multiple heading of trains as loads increased. On many occasions, four engines were needed for the trains and it is recorded that on one occasion, no fewer than seven of Bury's little engines were needed to pull a single goods train. But though they were too small and too feeble, Bury's engines were excellently made and their sound construction allowed them to carry on for a while. Eventually, in 1845, the year during which Bury first permitted Wolverton to manufacture its own locomotives (still four-wheelers), he also bowed to the inevitable and produced his first six-wheelers; but his influence was fast waning and, when the LNWR was formed in 1846, he resigned.

As an interesting side-line to the story of Bury's bar-framed engines, it is perhaps worth recording that although finding little favour in Britain, the bar frame concept was taken up with great enthusiasm in North America where it was developed to an astonishing degree, lasting right to the end of steam development on that continent – so maybe the L&BR

can be given a modicum of influence across the Atlantic as well.

Meantime, Bury was succeeded at Wolverton by J.E. McConnell, formerly of the Birmingham and Gloucester Railway. It is perhaps slightly surprising that Bury's resignation was not made the opportunity to amalgamate the locomotive affairs of the new LNWR under one man from the outset but for the next fifteen years, the GJR and L&BR sections of the line pursued their own courses in terms of locomotive development. Thus, McConnell was placed in charge of the Southern Division, as the L&BR was now called, and inherited a somewhat thankless task in terms of providing the L&BR with adequate locomotive power.

His appointment coincided with a decision by the LNWR to make everything within its own workshops in the interests

In early days during its search for a satisfactory type, the Southern (ex-L&BR) Division of the LNWR managed to acquire a number of alternatives to the Bury style. Locomotive No. LNWR 914 was of the Stephenson 'Long-Boiler' 0–6–0 type (ie firebox to the rear of the trailing axle) built by Fairburn and Sons in 1858 for the South Staffordshire Railway; it lasted until 1881 and was quite substantially proportioned for its time.

of greater economy. This was in due time to lead to the already mentioned rationalisation of roles between Crewe and Wolverton, but when McConnell took charge, the motive power situation was too acute for the policy to take immediate effect. In consequence, while he was working out his own locomotive designs for building at Wolverton, McConnell was allowed to purchase locomotives from elsewhere to hold the fort. All manner of designs were procured, most of them conventional enough, but one particularly interesting consequence of this period does merit mention, partly in relation to McConnell's quite different approach when new LNWR designs were introduced a few years later, but also in relation to the rapidly changing demands on the steam locomotive itself. This was the purchase by the LNWR of two of the (at the time quite celebrated) Crampton type locomotives.

At this time, considerable concern was beginning to develop about the stability of steam locomotives at the higher speeds beginning to develop and some engineers felt that to place the boiler too high above the rails contributed to the problem. This was an issue more or less confined to the standard gauge lines and was part of an attempt by them to increase speeds to those already attainable on the GWR with its inherently greater stability because of the broader gauge. It was a source of some irritation to the standard gauge fraternity and many ideas were tried out, none of which were really necessary on the broad gauge.

The main problem was boiler size, because if it was set low (to keep the centre of gravity down) then it had to fit, at least partially, between the driving wheels, and its diameter was thereby constrained. To give greater power, one could, of course, always make the boiler longer and add more wheels (the inadequacies of Bury's earlier engines had already demonstrated this fact) but there is always a critical technical relationship between boiler length and diameter, and situations could arise where one might well need both a longer and *larger diameter* boiler; the latter requirement could work against the low centre of gravity theory, since more of it would need to be mounted above the wheels. To make the wheels smaller in compensation was no real solution either since they would then need to rotate much faster to give the same running speed. This in turn would cause all the moving parts of the engine to work more rapidly than current 'state of the art' metallurgy and lubrication allowed. Indeed, for a high speed locomotive, large wheels were considered *de rigueur* by almost all engineers, largely to keep down the speed of movement of the working parts. The further possibility of increasing the steam pressure within the boiler to gain extra power without increase of boiler size was also generally disliked.

Thomas Crampton's solution to the problem, actually first patented as early as 1842, was highly ingenious in that he mounted a single huge pair of driving wheels to the rear of the boiler which could thus be set at a lower height between the carrying wheels ahead of the drivers than it could if the latter were in their conventional position. The most famous such example on the L&BR section was the celebrated *Liverpool*, a veritable Behemoth for its time (1848) with 8ft diameter wheels, over 2000 sq ft of boiler heating surface and a rare 6-2-0 wheel arrangement. Most Cramptons were 4-2-0s but *Liverpool*, the largest Crampton ever built, needed the extra pair of carrying wheels. It managed to move its trains at very

high speeds for the time (79mph being reported on one occasion), fully up to GWR standards, but its lengthy, rigid wheelbase was not kind to the track.

By now it will be appreciated that the demands of the new trunk railways were putting immense pressure on locomotive engineers to develop their ideas as rapidly as possible and nowhere was this more true than on the new-formed LNWR. At Wolverton, the company now had a man equal to the task and in 1851–2 McConnell rather staggered contemporary thought by producing a series of new engines which defied many accepted tenets of locomotive design, including some of those still in vogue at Crewe! They were six-wheel inside cylinder 2-2-2s of conventional enough configuration based very much on Bury's final six-wheelers, but had boilers operating at no less than 150psi in later examples – a well-nigh unheard of value for the time – set high above 7ft driving wheels and with inside plate frames only. They were a radical innovation compared with most contemporary engines and this fact is generally reckoned to be the reason for their instant nickname: 'Bloomers' – a somewhat obvious reference to an equally radical new type of ladies' garment introduced by Lady Emilia Bloomer at much the same time!

They were instantly successful and were eventually followed by a version with 6ft 6in driving wheels, thus creating 'Small Bloomers' and 'Large Bloomers'. Furthermore, McConnell's goods engines were equally sound and by contemporary standards, the Southern Division of the LNWR became a 'big engine' line during the 1850s and memories of the inadequately powered Bury days soon receded. However, this influence was not to permeate the whole of the LNWR; at Crewe they did things differently and it is to here we must now turn.

The 'Crewe' type (above) proved its worth in no uncertain manner and many indeed were built, generally 2-2-2s for passenger work and 2-4-0s for freight, but Francis Trevithick, who, incidentally, was the son of the actual inventor of the steam locomotive, did not, during the 1850s, share McConnell's enthusiasm for large engines and while Wolverton was busily thinking 'big', Trevithick and Alexander Allan went to the opposite extreme. Not for them the 7ft or occasionally, even 7ft 6in wheels of the Southern Division, 6ft wheels were considered quite adequate for an express engine. Moreover, whereas McConnell would regularly use big boilers capable of supplying adequate steam for 16in or even 18in diameter cylinders whose stroke was 22in or 24in, small boilers feeding 15in diameter by 20in stroke cylinders were usually sufficient to satisfy the Northern Division. The engines themselves were rugged and reliable but such divergence in approach to locomotive design between the two halves of the LNWR cannot have been conducive to efficiency. Some form of rationalisation was clearly required and in due course, took place; but not until Trevithick and McConnell had both gone.

The unifying force turned out to be yet another great locomotive engineer, John Ramsbottom. He had been in charge of locomotive affairs on the Manchester and Birmingham line from 1842 to its absorption into the LNWR in 1846 and, in that year, just as with the L&BR, the M&BR became a separate North Eastern Division within the new company, Ramsbottom continuing in charge of locomotives at Longsight, Manchester. When Trevithick retired in 1857,

The Crampton experiment on the L&BR is represented here by No.189, believed to be at Birmingham Curzon Street, c.1850.

These two pictures show 'Large' and 'Small' wheeled 'Bloomers', Nos.313 and 103, built for the Southern (ex-L&BR) division of the LNWR in 1854 and 1857 respectively. They were probably photographed c.1855 and 1861 and the latter picture of an engine built at Wolverton – a very celebrated Victorian image of the railway, by the way – was probably taken at Camden Loco. By any standards, these machines were much more 'puissant' locomotives than anything built at Crewe during the same period and were developed further during the post-McConnell regime of the LNWR.

This pair of commemorative LNWR postcard images gives a most useful and effective comparison between the 'Crewe' rebuilds of the 7ft driving wheel Wolverton 'Bloomers', exemplified by No. 1007 *President*, and the contemporary Ramsbottom 7ft 6in outside-cylindered 2–2–2s, represented here by No. 531 *Lady of the Lake* herself.

PASSENGER ENGINE "PRESIDENT"
BUILT 1861. DRIVING WHEELS 7FT. DIAMETER.

Exhibited at the International Exhibition in London in 1862 and awarded the bronze medal for excellence of workmanship. Has run 1 153,544 miles to end of Sept., 1904.

"LADY OF THE LAKE"
BUILT 1862. REBUILT 1876 & 1895.
DRIVING WHEELS 7FT. 6IN. DIAMETER.

the Northern and North Eastern Divisions were, sensibly and logically, amalgamated under John Ramsbottom, who then moved to Crewe. At this time, McConnell at Wolverton was the senior locomotive man and undoubtedly building more appropriately sized locomotives for the LNWR than was Trevithick at Crewe. History does not tell us whether McConnell ever expected to assume the mantle for the whole company; if he had, then things might have turned out rather differently. But there is some evidence that his engines were too expensive for some of the LNWR directors' liking.

Whatever the precise reasons, McConnell retired in 1861 and the Southern Division was finally amalgamated with the Northern Division in 1862 with John Ramsbottom in sole charge. Wolverton ceased its locomotive building activity and all new locomotive construction was henceforward concentrated at Crewe. By this time, Ramsbottom had already made his influence felt at Crewe and began to move it

away from the earlier 'small engine' philosophy. As early as 1858 he produced his first new LNWR express design, the celebrated 'Lady of the Lake' Class 2–2–2 engines whose basic dimensions were much closer to McConnells 'Bloomers' than anything hitherto built at Crewe, save for the maverick rebuild of Trevithick's *Cornwall*, originally put into service as an experimental design during the 'low centre of gravity' days with its boiler mostly below the driving axle! As rebuilt – and now preserved – this is basically a very large 'Crewe' type.

Ramsbottom's 'Ladies' shared the high-boilered configuration of the 'Large Bloomers' and had even bigger wheels (7ft 6in), but still had typically Crewe style outside cylinders. These were no longer enclosed between double frames at the front but the engines retained the gracefully curved smokebox wrapper of the classic 'Crewe' type and it may have seemed for a while as if the outside cylinder type was destined to continue as a Crewe standard. But the 'Ladies' were to be the last new outside-cylindered engines to be built at Crewe for many a long year.

Excellent and long-lived though the 'Ladies' were and very popular with their crews, all other Ramsbottom designs were of the by now conventionally orthodox inside cylindered type, not dissimilar in fact to those already being built by McConnell at Wolverton. They had wholly inside frames and the first of them actually appeared in the same year as the 'Ladies', far less glamorous in conception but far more numerous and vastly more revenue earning. They were goods engines of the 0–6–0 type, known as the DX Class and in time, no fewer than 943 of them were built at Crewe, almost certainly the largest class of identical engines ever built for use on a British main line. Ramsbottom had started the LNWR onto its soon-to-become familiar policy of mass-producing but a few different and essentially simple types of locomotive to operate the ever increasing traffic on what was now beginning to be called Britain's Premier Line.

Nevertheless, Wolverton's contribution was of greater significance than outward appearances suggested. McConnell had not only pioneered larger engines (a concept adopted by Ramsbottom) but they were far better than his departure from the scene may have suggested. In due course, Crewe took over maintenance of the whole of the LNWR locomotive fleet as well as its construction and, when this phase was well established, those non-Crewe built types with anything like a reasonable life-expectancy were soon assimilated to the mainstream of company styling by virtue of being rebuilt with what were now LNWR standard components. Thus, McConnell's robustly built 'Bloomers' and 0–6–0 goods engines began to sport Crewe pattern cabs, boilers and boiler fittings and before very long, they began to take on visual characteristics very similar to the 'home made' product.

It was at this time, roughly about 1870, that the purely L&BR needs in terms of locomotive evolution finally gave way to those of the greater system of which it formed a part and, of course, it has continued thus ever since. In 1871, Ramsbottom retired, having in but ten years set the LNWR on a course of locomotive evolution which it followed faithfully for the best part of half a century. For over thirty of those years, until 1903, the locomotive destiny of the LNWR lay in the hands of but one man, Francis William Webb, one of the most misunderstood yet arguably also one of the greatest locomotive engineers of all time. Under his guidance, the LNWR developed what was probably the greatest company-owned locomotive manufacturing capability anywhere in the

The astonishing similarity between McConnell's Wolverton-built 0–6–0 5ft 6-in wheeled goods locomotives and the Ramsbottom 5ft 3in DX Class 0–6–0s from Crewe is well shown in this pair of pictures showing Southern Division No.371 (1861) and Crewe-built No.454 (1870).

This Ramsbottom DX 0–6–0 No.1420 of 1865, rebuilt by Webb as a 'Special DX' in 1894, shows possibly the most characteristic 'LNWR' image of these most celebrated engines.

world. And its products were instantly recognisable anywhere.

Webb built on the fine foundations laid by Ramsbottom and simply developed them in the simplest and most economical way possible. Put like that it sounds simple, but it must be viewed against a contemporary background wherein most other railways felt it needful to change their designs regularly and frequently, sometimes on not much more than a 'keeping up with the Joneses' basis. Webb could see no virtue in this. His remit was to provide engines to make money for the company shareholders and the LNWR geared itself up to do just this. It was in all probability the first company to realise fully the considerable monetary virtues of large scale standardisation and although its engines may not have been the most sophisticated or efficient ever built, they surely were amongst the most cost-effective in terms of initial capital outlay. Moreover, Webb's influence at Crewe ensured that they could be built at a prodigiously fast rate; the LNWR rapidly outstripped all other British companies in terms of numbers of locomotives built in its own shops and by the time the last new steam engine came out of Crewe, it was leading the British field by many thousands. This was the lasting achievement of Francis Webb; but on the way he also caused to be built some remarkably good engines as well.

Towards the end of his period in office, Ramsbottom had designed a simply conceived inside frame and inside cylindered 2–4–0 express passenger type known as the 'Newton' Class. This was the true harbinger of all that was to become most celebrated about LNWR locomotives during the Webb era, not least most of the company's visual lines which were 'set' for almost half a century. Webb developed the 'Newtons' into his own 'Precedent' Class which for some 20 years or more was, in its various developments, the mainstay of LNWR express workings. They called them all 'Jumbos', conceivably because of the prodigious amount of work they did and those who have seen the preserved *Hardwicke* at the National Railway Museum can continue to marvel at the apparently diminutive size of these hard-working machines. It is still hard to credit that this little engine could have run with a train from Crewe to Carlisle in 1895 in a time which would not entirely shame a modern electric!

In these engines, Webb took great care that amongst all the simplicity and desired cheapness of construction, the design was sound where it mattered. In the case of the 2–4–0s, which would be expected to work hard – that being the LNWR way of doing things – it was vitally important that the steam flow through the cylinders was not impeded. Webb gave it plenty of space to get in and out of the cylinders quickly and this

Ramsbottom 'Newton' Class 2–4–0 No.1679 *Bunsen* of 1868 represented one of the truly seminal stages in the evolution of LNWR express motive power on the L&BR and West Coast routes.

The Immortal Webb 'Jumbo' 2–4–0s, here represented by an unidentified example in the London suburbs heading south during late LNWR days, were almost certainly the most outstanding locomotives designed by this celebrated LNWR engineer.

meant that the engines could be driven at almost full throttle whenever required. The basic principle was traceable back to the 'Bloomers' and they were thrashed along at a time when other railways were tending to make bigger engines, but the LNWR dividend was kept at the sort of levels which eventually saw it grow into the largest joint stock corporation in the world – a veritable 'blue chip' investment.

But if the 'Jumbos' were perhaps Webb's finest design – and they did work the best trains right to the turn of the century – he also made ample provision for the most financially remunerative part of his railway's activity – freight haulage. Like Ramsbottom, he caused to be built many hundreds of what, without any insult to them, may safely be called 'cheap and cheerful' 0–6–0s, basically to only two designs. There were small wheeled 'coal' engines for mineral and other slow moving and/or heavy traffic and there were larger (5ft 3in) wheeled engines for the faster moving traffic – the 'Express Goods Engines' as they were called. These were sometimes called 'Crested Goods' because, alone of the LNWR goods engines at the time, they carried the proud LNWR 'Britannia' crest on their splashers. The enginemen thought the crest looked a bit like a cauliflower so 'Cauliflowers' they soon became – the LNWR rather liked nicknames!

Webb 'Cauliflower' 0–6–0, now LMS No.8441, still going strong on Camden bank in 1936.

Just as Ramsbottom had done with his 0–6–0s, Webb produced tank engine variants of all these tender types for shorter distances (most commonly of the 0–6–2T or 2–4–2T wheel arrangement) and all shared many parts in common with his other designs in the interests of economic manufacturing and maintenance. Webb was also one of the first British engineers to move to the eight–wheeled 0–8–0 type freight engine when loads exceeded the capability of the 0–6–0 and, of course, it was he who decided, as early as 1873, that all LNWR engines should be painted black, again in the interest of economy. Hitherto, Crewe had used green and Wolverton mostly green but latterly red. Yet again, Webb could see no virtue in spending more money on paint than was needful to protect the metal work; black was cheapest so black the engines became, but what a black! In due time it became just as famous as many of the more colourful schemes adopted by other railways and when it was polished to perfection by a devoted footplate crew, as was many times the case, there was no smarter turnout in the land than LNWR 'Blackberry' black. And there was also some light relief in the often bizarre names which the LNWR bestowed on its express engines with such gay abandon.

Webb was also a great organisation chief and worked veritable miracles at Crewe where, in time, he took on something like demi-god status. Furthermore, such was the reputation of the LNWR that to be a locomotive apprentice under Webb was considered to be the finest training to be obtained anywhere. Amongst the many famous men who trained under him one need perhaps only mention Sir Nigel Gresley – eventually to design the world's fastest steam locomotive – to realise his lasting influence.

All this achievement and much more stands attributable to Webb, yet the fact is that he left the LNWR in 1903 in a state bordering on discredit and many later writers have given him a poor press ever since. It was manifestly unfair and stemmed from the one, relatively small, area in which he was less than successful, his latter day experimentation with compound steam propulsion.

In a compound steam locomotive, the steam is used twice, once at full boiler pressure and then, after leaving the high pressure cylinder(s), it does not exhaust up the chimney as in a simple engine but is re-used in one or more lower pressure cylinders prior to its eventual exhaust up the chimney in the conventional manner. This makes more use of the expansive property of steam, thus leading to economy and more efficient use of fuel and water, but at some cost in greater mechanical complexity. Theoretically, the compound is a better solution in terms of steam locomotive design than the traditional Stephenson simple engine and it is a matter of fact that the most efficient designs, both thermodynamically and in terms of power to weight ratio, have been compounds – mostly designed by the French by the way. Webb probably knew

The Webb 2–4–2Ts lasted for much longer than their more exalted main line contemporaries. Here is LMS No.6635, still in pretty fair shape at Bletchley in 1946.

some of this and the promised economies of compounding must have appealed to him, especially when set against the frugally prudent financial policies of the LNWR.

Unfortunately, Webb never managed to get the technical 'mix' quite right in any of his many compound types. He made many separate attempts, whose various differences need not concern us here since they are all well recorded in other technical sources; and they were by no means always bad. For example, his three-cylinder 'Teutonic' design (two high press-ure outside cylinders and one extremely large low pressure inside cylinder) was a very 'near-miss'. These designs had their two sets of driving wheels driven separately, the leading pair by the low pressure cylinder and the rear pair by the high pressure cylinders. They looked somewhat like large versions of the 'Jumbo' 2–4–0s, but having no coupling rods between their driving wheels, they were more correctly described as 2–2–2–0s and there are several, probably apocryphal, tales of them trying to start out from Euston with the two pairs of driving wheels trying to rotate in opposite directions! It may have happened once or twice but cannot have been a serious problem since one of the 'Teutonics', named *Jeanie Deans*, achieved an almost ever-present status for some ten years on

the famous 2pm 'Corridor' train, hardly an indicator of a totally bad design.

Some of his later four-cylinder effects were quite reasonable and did some useful work but other compounds were, by any standards, quite execrable and not well liked. One particular feeble class – 4–6–0s as it so happened – were instantly christened 'Bill Baileys', a less than flattering allusion to the fact that they rarely managed to 'come home' without atten-tion. Inevitably the result of the failure led to all Webb's experiments in the compound genre becoming suspect and the passage of time has overlain all of Webb's genuine achievements with the opprobium gained by his compounds. The real irony is that, in numerical terms, the compound engines accounted for a relatively small proportion of the total he built during his term in office.

It was singularly unfortunate that Webb's compound experiments coincided with the need to increase engine power, consequent upon the large and heavier new carriages and the ever-increasing size of goods trains. It seems not unfair to conclude that, with his compounds, Webb was trying to get this extra power with improved economy as well – a not unreasonable aim in purely commercial terms –and he

69

certainly moved away from the six-wheel engine to something large during this period. The 4–6–0 has been mentioned but there were also some eight-wheeled passenger engines (4–4–0s and 2–2–2–2s) plus both 0–8–0 and 2–8–0 goods engines. But it was all to no avail. Webb was by now quite an old man, some even considered him to be approaching a form of senility and there is little doubt that there was 'back stairs' agitation to have him removed from office. In due course, he left under something of a cloud in 1903 – a sad ending.

Such was the reputation of Crewe during Webb's days, however, that the fact that even the mighty LNWR could not make successful compounds had the not entirely happy consequence that the compound steam locomotive was, for the most part, blighted for ever more in the eyes of most British railways, and this was a pity. The significant improvements in steam locomotive development mostly moved away from Britain during the 20th Century and the compound was very much a part of this improvement. It is therefore at least arguable that just as the LNWR had been almost globally influential in the 19th Century, its failure to move forward at the end of the Webb era had more than a little to do with the relative insularity which thereafter overtook most British steam locomotive development.

Webb's compound experiments embraced quite a variety of types. One of the rather more successful was the four-cylinder 4–4–0 type seen here at Camden in June 1901 in the form of No.1919 *King Arthur*. Later developments decreed that most of these engines were rebuilt to two-cylinder simple form; as such, *King Arthur* survived until 1930. A 'Cauliflower' 0–6–0 is also seen in the background of this view.

Amongst the more successful of the Webb compounds were his eight-coupled goods engines, probably because high speed was the least important of their attributes. No.1432 was a 'B' Class 0–8–0, built in 1904 (after Webb had left the LNWR) but even this late-built example was eventually (1922) rebuilt to simple form and as such, survived until 1948 as LMS No.9384.

Webb was replaced by George Whale – a 'running' man – and he felt that what the line really needed was more of the old fashioned simple stuff, as represented by the 'Jumbos', but rather bigger. In consequence, his first two express designs ('Precursor' 4–4–0s and the near-identical 'Experiment' 4–6–0s, with somewhat smaller driving wheels for greater adhesive weight on the steeper sections of the line north of Crewe) were, at first sight, little more than enlarged Webb 2–4–0s. This is, in fact, a slight over-simplification, there were other changes too; but as far as the enginemen were concerned, they were again given engines which could have the living daylights thrashed out of them and pull prodigiously heavy trains compared with their Webb forebears. In consequence they were delighted and Whale rapidly either scrapped the compounds or (in the case of the later 4–4–0s and most of the eight-coupled goods engines) rebuilt them to the simple and familiar inside cylinder form, a process which continued for many years thereafter.

Whale was in office for only six years but he virtually turned the LNWR round as far as the locomotive crisis was concerned and was followed in the same vein by the last of the 'great' LNWR locomotive engineers, Charles John Bowen Cooke. Cooke introduced superheating to otherwise pretty well unchanged Whale designs. Superheating was a continental innovation which, expressed at its simplest, was a method by which the boiler steam could be further heated before passing to the cylinders. This had the effect of still further increasing its expansive power and eliminating the possibility of the steam condensing back to liquid form before completing its working cycle. It required better lubrication but gave considerable fuel economy compared with a 'saturated' engine. If truth be told, Britain was a bit slow to adopt the idea and it was not until the LNWR had actually borrowed and tested a superheated 4–4–2T from the London Brighton and South Coast Railway (of all companies!) that Cooke was finally convinced of the virtues of superheated steam.

Superheating seemed to confer all the theoretical advantages of a compound without any of its concomitant complications – in fact, a properly designed and *superheated* compound could give a double benefit but few in Britain listened (!) – and Bowen Cooke adopted superheat with enthusiasm. In so doing, he produced one minor masterpiece, one very near miss and laid the foundations for a fine series of heavy freight engines which the even greater William Stanier saw fit to continue to develop throughout the LMS period.

Bowen Cooke's superheated 'George the Fifth' LNWR 4–4–0s of 1910 can lay sound claim to have been one of the most outstanding locomotive designs of the pre-1914 era. They regularly horsed,unassisted, 4–500 ton loads out of Euston – a performance unmatched by any other British design save for the much larger locomotives of GWR and GNR design – and were thrashed to the limit by crews only too pleased to show the mettle of their charges. It was hardly surprising that when the LMS got them they were a bit weary, but even in King George VI's Coronation year of 1937, No.5348, having been named in honour of his father's similar event of 1911, could still put on a brave show at the special Euston event to celebrate the later occasion.

Bowen Cooke's 'near-miss': an elegant 'Claughton' Class 4–6–0, now running as LMS No.5998, seen here at Wembley in 1934 in charge of an up express of somewhat indeterminate parentage!

Cooke's greatest achievement was his superheated 'George the Fifth' Class, developed from Whale's 'Precursor' 4–4–0. These amazing engines regularly hauled 4–500 ton trains from Euston unassisted when most comparably sized engines on other lines could be hard-pressed with not much more than half that load at the same speed. For almost 20 years, they and their 4–6–0 equivalent (the 'Prince of Wales' Class) bore the brunt of LNWR services and many of the 'Precursors' were superheated to match them. The 4–6–0 version, though not

perhaps quite as good in the absolute sense, was somewhat more versatile in terms of its suitability for other traffic and was built in quantity throughout the rest of the LNWR period, eventually totalling 245 machines, to which total the LMS added a final example. It became, in fact if not in name, the LNWR version of the later and ubiquitous 'mixed traffic' locomotive of the post-grouping period.

Bowen Cooke's near-miss was the elegant four-cylinder 4–6–0 'Sir Gilbert Claughton' Class, a superheated express engine for the heaviest duties. When 'on song' and in good order they were magnificent, but their boilers were too small; that was the fault of the civil engineer who would not allow a greater axle weight to be carried, being unaware (or unconvinced) that because its rotating masses were better balanced, a four-cylinder engine did far less damage to the track than did a lighter two-cylinder machine – such was the stuff of railways in those days and it worked to the benefit of no-one. But the Claughtons also suffered from some quite typical Crewe detail defects, in particular poor lubrication; in due course, this prevented them from being the outright winners which potentially they could have been.

The final purely LNWR contribution to locomotive development – and perhaps the most important in strict revenue terms – was the superheated 0–8–0 goods engine, developed

The final significant LNWR contribution to British locomotive affairs came in the form of the rebuilt, belpaire-boilered 0–8–0s, represented here by No.9413, northbound at Bourne End in 1935.

essentially by progressive enlargement (and the abandonment of compounding) from Webb's early experiments. Whale had started the process with the 'D Class' by fitting a large boiler to older Webb engines but Cooke, in his superheated 'G1 Class' of 1912, came up with the real winner. This was evolved into the G2 version before grouping and during LMS days, well over 500 0–8–0s assumed this superheated form. There were several quite subtle differences between them but all were most familiarly known as 'Super Ds', a reference to the fact that the first G1 was a *super*heated conversion of the old 'D Class'. Their successful transformation must have saved the LMS many thousands of pounds and may well have delayed the need for building too many further heavy freight engines until well into the Stanier period.

If truth be told, however, no matter how effectively Whale and Cooke had overcome the post-Webb problems, the LNWR, in its final years, was no longer the prime force in locomotive evolution which it had been in the 19th Century. It did, of course, continue to command great respect and pay its dividends to the end, but it was to be more than a generation after Webb had left, and under a quite different influence, that Crewe and its products again began to achieve the sort of significance which it had always tended to regard as its right!

The story actually started on the GWR at Swindon, which adopted the third basic type of conventional steam locomotive

– broad gauge 'Patentees' – from an early stage. But the broad gauge was always doomed to failure because of its incompatibility with the through running of vehicles to the rest of the country. The standard gauge was by far the more common and the GWR eventually completed the conversion of its lines to the Stephensonian 4ft 8½in in 1892. This gave it a unique and once for all chance to start again with locomotive evolution and after a period of some ten or twenty years, during which William Dean oversaw the first stages of the transition to the new order, there came onto the scene at Swindon, a man in the F. W. Webb mould, but with all the understanding of modern locomotive developments which seemed missing at Crewe. His name, of course, was George Jackson Churchward.

Churchward immediately initiated a high degree of standardisation of parts and practices at Swindon – that was nothing new, Crewe had been doing it for a generation – but Churchward combined this with a more profound understanding of the fundamental steam locomotive itself than anyone else in the country. Drawing heavily on contemporary American and French practice, he launched the GWR into a new era with a series of radically different locomotive designs which were, in terms of both performance and thermo-dynamic efficiency, 'light years' ahead of most other British railways. They looked different and they were different – and far more sophisticated than their competitors. They were also expensive to make by comparison with those of other lines, especially the LNWR, and this gave rise to some amusing incidents.

It is said that Churchward, when challenged by his Board of Directors as to why his engines cost far more to build than those of the LNWR, stated that it was because 'One of mine will pull two of their bloody things backwards!', or some such. Whether this be true or not is largely irrelevant, but in 1910, an exchange between the two companies was arranged and a GWR four-cylinder 4–6–0 No. 4005 *Polar Star* was sent to the LNWR in exchange for a non-superheated 'Experiment' Class 4–6–0 No. 1471 *Worcestershire*. It was really 'no contest' and the GWR came away feeling well pleased. Bowen Cooke may not have been too displeased either since he could have a good look at the 'Star' which, conceptually, was not dissimilar from his own proposed 'Claughton' 4–6–0. However, it might have been very different had the LNWR been fully alert!

Churchward maintained that a two-ton 'pull' at 70mph was a suitable target for a modern express engine and his own machines could do just that. What he did not seem to appreciate – and Crewe did not bother to tell him – was that the superheated LNWR 'George the Fifth' 4–4–0 could equal this achievement at far less capital cost; there are too many performance figures on record to be in any real doubt on this score. To the writer, it has always been a source of some astonishment that the LNWR did not put up a 'George' against the 'Star' but such it was and, for many years afterwards, Churchward's reputation and that of the GWR, reigned supreme. Interestingly, Churchward's one failing, if thus it may be called, was his lack of appreciation of the virtues of a fully superheated locomotive. He did employ a form of superheat, but this was little more than a form of 'steam drying' and this was eventually to have interesting consequences at Crewe.

In all other respects, Churchward represented a model which all could envy. In particular, his strength lay in his meticulous attention to detail design, an insistence on a very high standard of workshop practice, close attention to the importance of driver training and, perhaps above all, a real appreciation of the fundamental importance in terms of economy and efficiency of good boiler and valve gear design (the latter being the means whereby steam is got into and out of the cylinders). It give the GWR a clear cut locomotive lead for the best part of a generation and such was the lack of real competition that in time there began to develop at Swindon the sort of complacency and self-satisfaction which had in an earlier day, been quite normal at Crewe. It had an equally adverse effect on the parent company for, in due course, Swindon's pioneering role was assumed by the old LNWR works and the instrument of this change was one of Swindon's own sons. His name was William Arthur Stanier and he took charge of LMS locomotive affairs, including responsibility for Crewe works, in 1932.

Before coming into Stanier's work on the LMS, however, it is necessary to review, if but briefly, the circumstances by which he came to be appointed; it is not unconnected with events at Crewe a decade earlier.

Bowen Cooke, sadly, died in 1920 before reaching his normal retirement age and was succeeded by the euphoniously named Captain Hewitt Pearson Montague Beames. Now Beames was an admirable man and, as events were to prove, one of Stanier's most loyal supporters, but he was no Bowen Cooke and his career was stifled by the consequences of the great amalgamations of the early 1920s in which seniority and 'pecking order' were perceived to be all important. Thus, when the LNWR amalgamated with the Lancashire and Yorkshire Railway in 1922, one year ahead of the main grouping, Beames was junior to George Hughes, the LYR Chief Engineer, who thereupon became the new man in charge.

This was not in itself any bad thing; Hughes himself was a fine engineer and probably second only to Churchward at the time. He was certainly one of the few who combined the

The highly successful 'Horwich' 2–6–0s held the fort for several years in the early LMS period. This is No.13112 of 1929.

virtues of high superheat with modern valve gear but he worked for a provincial railway and, in consequence, does not always seem to have been given his due share of credit. He was also the most senior man when the LMS was formed and became the first CME of the new company. However, he was by now near to retirement and seems to have been quite prepared to settle for a quiet life at Horwich (the old LYR Locomotive works) rather than get involved with the mainly 'political' in-fighting which was to bedevil the early days of the new LMS. And in-fighting there was – in plenty! However, Hughes can take most of the credit for the first entirely new LMS locomotive design – an excellent mixed traffic 2–6–0 – which emerged in 1926, a year after he retired; it was one of the relatively few good things to emerge in those troubled days.

Beames was again passed over in 1926, being also junior to the ex-Midland Railway CME, Sir Henry Fowler. In consequence, Midland policies now began to assume even greater dominance than they had in 1923 when the LMS management had found itself heavily influenced by the ex-MR contingent (seniority again, of course!). Now the Midland was in many

In time, the Midland compounds settled down to some good work, even on the ex-LNWR lines, but double-heading was still rife. In this view No. 1111 pilots an unidentified Stanier Class 5XP 'Jubilee' 4–6–0 on a northbound express south of Watford in the mid-1930s, a time when even with 'Royal Scot' 4–6–0s and Stanier 4–6–2s, the LMS was still 'pushed' for power.

An early LMS endeavour to produce a heavy duty freight locomotive was a marriage of the superheated LNWR 0–8–0 boiler with a Midland-inspired chassis incorporating quite modern valve gear. The resultant Class 7F 0–8–0 was an 'iffish' sort of creation, not quite in the top flight but by no means as bad as some would aver. This view shows No.9508, northbound at Northchurch in 1935 with an empty coal train.

respects a most admirable company but its preferred management methods, appropriate to its own role, did not transfer easily to the new amalgamated LMS and, in particular, they proved something of a major disaster on the locomotive front. The Midland preferred to use small engines, run lightly-loaded passenger trains and double-head anything whenever loads began, even marginally, to stretch the capacity of a single engine. These ideas were anathema to the LNWR. Furthermore, the best Midland express engine was a modest sized 4–4–0 (at a time when most railways had gone for something bigger) and when the LMS began to draft dozens of new examples onto the LNWR lines they went down like lead balloons. The fact that they were painted in the 'enemy' colours of red, and were *compounds* to boot, did not help either – memories of Webb died hard. It was, in truth, a little unfair to the Midland compound, for it was the best such design ever built in quantity by a British railway but, even discounting the compound aspect, it must be said that they were, overall, too small in absolute terms for the main line needs of the new LMS.

The Crewe-versus-Derby conflict continued for many years – there was also a Scottish element to add some Gaelic piquancy to the LMS sauce – and it must have seemed at times as though there could never be any reconciliation between the disparate parties. During the which while, some progress was made on the locomotive front – and not a little dross emerged as well. Crewe was reorganised, largely due to the splendid efforts of Hewitt Beames, but overall, the new LMS needed strong central management and a real sense of purpose. It is a matter of history that it got it, the instrument of change being an economist, Sir Josiah Stamp, later Lord Stamp of Short-lands who, after his appointment in 1925, dragged his management, reluctant and screaming at times, into the 20th Century. It took him a few years to get everything into place, but without him it is all but certain that William Stanier would never have been appointed; in which case the course of British locomotive development would almost certainly have taken on a very different form.

In the late 20th Century, we are accustomed to the role of huge industrial corporations, often of a multi-national kind, but in the context of inter-war Britain, Lord Stamp's LMS was something quite new and went a long way to set the pattern of present-day company management. In truth, however, it was not too different, conceptually, from such earlier giants as the LNWR. One senses that Richard Moon and Francis Webb would not have felt entirely out of place at Josiah Stamp's meetings. Above all, he lacked sentiment. The railway was a commercial organisation whose job was not only to give a service but also to make money. This had, of course, always been true but, in the 1920s and 1930s, times were actually different and more difficult than in the 19th Century, if only because of increased competition from the roads and later, even the air. Thus, as far as Stamp was concerned, locomotives were energy conversion devices whose sole task was to move traffic as expeditiously as possible at the lowest cost. This implied a combination of standardisation and efficiency. The economic advantage of the first was determined long before Stanier came on the scene by Stamp's introducing a system of accurate locomotive costing which revealed that new standard locomotives, of whatever design, actually cost less to keep running than patching up the old-timers. This determined, Stamp only needed to find the person who could make the most *efficient* standard engines; William Stanier was his chosen man.

There is some evidence that Stanier was, in fact, 'poached' from the GWR, but he seems to have been a willing victim! He was only a few years younger than his immediate GWR chief, C.B. Collett and would therefore be unlikely to inherit the Swindon mantle; but his credentials were impeccable. He had been Churchward's works manager at Swindon and therefore knew the virtues of good workshop practice and standardisation – an aspect not unknown at Crewe either – but he also could be expected to know something of Churchward's other 'secrets' as well in terms of more refined design and detail improvements. Thus, one supposes, Stamp concluded that in William Stanier he had the right man to fuse all the best elements of his former railway with those of his new company, to the major benefit of the latter. This was largely the case and during the 1930s and afterwards, the

successors to the old London and Birmingham Railway once again assumed the pre-eminent role first cast for them by Robert Stephenson.

Those of Stanier's team who had suffered the nonsenses of the first ten years of the LMS period must have been mightily glad to get away from the dog-fighting and back to the business of making locomotives. Possibly of most significance, he had the full backing of Crewe works. Whatever the failings of the LNWR in terms of refined locomotive design, it possessed in Crewe works one of the most outstanding locomotive manufacturing establishments anywhere in the world, with a quite extraordinary capability for 'can do' and improvisation. It is said that Stanier had no great regard for Crewe when he joined the LMS but soon had to 'eat his words' when he fully appreciated the quality of its workmanship, especially in the all-important business of boiler making. The key man here was Hewitt Beames.

Thrice pased over after the death of Bowen Cooke, four times if one counts the brief interregnum of Ernest Lemon in 1931 between Fowler and Stanier, Beames could have been forgiven in purely human terms had he simply decided that enough was enough and retired gracefully; but no, the old

This identically posed trio of views at Bourne End in 1935 shows the fundamental gestation of the mid-powered LMS 5XP express passenger type in Pre-Stanier days. It started with the 'Royal Scots' of 1927 which established the 3–cylinder chassis layout (No.6142 *Lion*, later *The York and Lancaster Regiment*). This was followed in 1928 by a larger boiler applied to the existing 4–cylinder LNWR 'Claughton Class' 4–6–0 (No.6004, formerly *Princess Louise*) and culminated in 1930 with the marriage of the new 'Claughton' boiler with the Royal Scot chassis to form the new 3–cylinder 5XP type (No.5542).

Stanier's most numerous early contributions to the LMS scene were his two series of 4–6–0s: the 'red' 3–cylinder 5XPs (a logical development of the earlier 'Patriots') and the 'black' 2–cylinder Class 5P5F engines (a new concept). In due time they came to epitomise the revitalised LMS scene and the London and Birmingham section came to know both types very well. In these views, 5XP No.5552 *Silver Jubilee* (the one exception to the 'red' rule, being finished in glossy black with chrome trimmings in 1935 to commemorate the 1935 Jubilee, thus giving 'Jubilee' nomenclature to the whole class) is seen southbound near Bushey with a short and motley, but typically LMS collection of assorted coaches. Perhaps typically, the 'black' 5, No.5174, southbound near Hatch End, has a much heavier and tidier train!

LNWR was made of sterner stuff and Beames wrote to Stanier on the latter's appointment: 'You will understand how disappointed I am, but I may say there is no one I would rather work under than you'. How many, I wonder, could write thus? But it ensured Crewe's wholehearted co-operation with the new order and provided Stanier with the means by which he could institute his necessary changes. Like it or not, Derby would take second place to Crewe in the Stanier period and this had some even more important consequences in the post-Stanier era.

Stanier's first years were not plain sailing. He had inherited Churchward's attitude towards superheating for example (see above) and was rather suprised to discover that Swindon boiler shapes and proportions, most visibly exemplified by the trapezoidal Belpaire firebox shape and tapered boiler barrel, did not always respond too well to the hurly-burly of typical LMS operating conditions, and the generally less cosseted nature of its engines compared with those of the GWR, unless they were married to a higher degree of superheat than Swindon felt needful. In a word, Stanier was faced with rather more of the reality of modern steam train operation in the

LMS of the 1930s than had ever been the case in Wiltshire! But he was quick to learn, his staff were intensely loyal to him and he himself was most approachable. It is one of my more proud boasts that I was privileged both to be friendly with and speak personally to two of Stanier's most devoted lieutenants, Robert Riddles and Roland Bond, in their twilight years and, to quote Riddles: 'Sir William was a marvellous Chief and I owe so much to him . . .' Riddles, of course, took over the Stanier mantle in BR in due course and was a die-hard LNWR man if ever I met one!

It should also be pointed out that neither Stanier nor his supporters ever claimed him to be the most innovative 20th Century British locomotive engineer; no patents stand to his name and, after Churchward, the mantle of innovation in the British context must surely be put on the shoulders of Sir Nigel Gresley, the celebrated locomotive supremo of the LNER during the 1930s. But Gresley was given his head in a way that Stamp's utterly practical LMS would never have countenanced – in fact, Gresley was virtually permitted by his company to act in the manner of a latter-day Brunel; so Stanier's achievement must be viewed in the light of the company he served. In this regard, the rivalry which still breaks out between enthusiastic followers of Gresley and Stanier is at one and the same time both irrelevant and futile; they were in fact, close personal friends with a high regard for each other's achievements; in any case, as has already been stated, Gresley trained under Webb at Crewe!

Stanier's lasting achievement is the way he fused the warring elements in the LMS into a locomotive team which stood supreme when he retired. The actual engines he designed are less relevant in this respect; in any case, they do not lack for literary coverage elsewhere. What he did was to translate the new LMS philosophy into operational 'hardware'. It was less glamorous than the role of some of his contemporaries but who can say it was less relevant? In but eleven short years (about the same time as it had taken John Ramsbottom to wreak the same transformation on the LNWR some 75 years previously) he transformed the LMS from laughing stock to national leader. His two largest standard classes, the Class 5 mixed traffic 4–6–0s and the heavy freight Class 8 2–8–0s, each represented by more than 800 examples,

produced the same sort of transformation of fortunes for his company as had the mass production of Ramsbottom's DX Class 0–6–0s in an earlier era. Furthermore, just as Ramsbottom had set the stage for Webb's continuation, so too did Stanier set the scene for almost the whole of the final phase of British steam locomotive development. In this respect, the more refined and sophisticated nuances of thermodynamic perfection had little part to play; Stanier was a practical man.

Nowhere was this more true than in the final steam locomotives built in Britain after the end of the company period of 31st December 1947. Stanier had by now retired from the LMS – he actually departed at the end of 1942 – but it is a measure of his stature that there remained little left to do of an innovative nature as far as his steam traction successors were concerned. There were, in fact, but three of them: C.M. Fairburn and H.G. Ivatt on the LMS and R.A. Riddles during the BR period.

Fairburn succeeded Stanier in 1943 but died tragically soon afterwards. He was essentially an electrical engineer, of which more anon, and his only real steam contribution was to

Above Left Although not built in any great quantity during the early days, Stanier's Class 8F 2-8-0 was ultimately to become the most numerous of his designs and saw the end of steam working on the BR system. This is No.48674 in its final years 'under the wires' at Willesden in August 1985. Above Right & Below The ultimate steam achievement on the L&BR/LNWR/LMS was undoubtedly Stanier's immortal 'Princess Coronation' Class 4-6-2 design of 1937, the most powerful express passenger type ever produced in Britain and never surpassed in performance tested scientifically. In these views, the prototype streamlined engine, LMS No.6220 Coronation is seen southbound near Watford on what is believed to be the return working of its record-breaking run in 1937, while in the second view non-streamlined BR No.46253 City of St Albans, built in 1946, heads south through Weedon towards London with the up 'Shamrock' express in April 1962.

modify Stanier's already excellent suburban 2–6–4T design to permit slightly greater route availability. Ivatt, son of the perhaps even more famous Henry Ivatt of the Great Northern Railway, merely carried Stanier's precepts to a more logical stage, that of providing new, modern and easily maintained locomotives for the sort of secondary services which had hitherto been performed by superannuated and often expensive to keep going pre-group types. He also initiated some experimental modifications to the basic Stanier types, including the final pair of immortal 'Duchess' type 4–6–2s, by any standards the most puissant express engines ever built for use in Britain, mainly to see whether further economic improvement could be gained. That there was very little real improvement to any of the designs so tackled is less to the discredit of Ivatt than it is evidence of the fundamental soundness of the original Stanier design.

The London and Birmingham Railway, now part of the greater LMS, gave way to the unified BR system in 1948 and it may reasonably be supposed that the specific needs of Robert Stephenson's original line would play a very minor part in future motive power development. In the literal sense this was, of course, true, but since the L&BR was the essential spinal cord of the LMS, its long term influence lived on at second hand, so to speak.

In the final days of steam traction, little of significance really changed. It is a measure of Stanier's stature that, notwithstanding the contributions of the other British railways to the story, his 'first' team was appointed, virtually undiluted, to take charge of motive power matters on the new BR system. Robert Riddles, Stanier's former personal assistant in the 1930s, was put in charge of affairs and although he did, wisely, take counsel elsewhere, there was no real denying the fact that the basic LMS philosophy would continue in the absence of anything better. In truth there was very little competition at the time. Gresley had died in office on the LNER in 1941 and his successors, especially Edward Thompson (1941–6) seemed to be doing their level best to imitate LMS methods (!), Bulleid on the Southern Railway was pursuing maverick and wildly impractical steam locomotive policies at odds with the reality of the 1940s, while the GWR had still not got over the shock either of nationalisation or the fact that one of its own men had taken Churchward's precepts far further than had happened at Swindon! All told it was game, set and match to the LMS team!

Thus it was that it fell to Robert Riddles, LNWR trained and the lineal descendant of both McConnell and Ramsbottom, not to mention Webb and Stanier, to see BR through the final phase of steam development. He could have simply continued with LMS designs – and Roland Bond told me that there was no good reason why not – but Riddles was a good psychologist. He well remembered the trauma of the 1920s when Midland Railway methods were inflicted without debate on a reluctant LMS, so he resolved on new designs. For the most part they were not strictly needed; most of the

Post-war utility: Ivatt 'Class 4' 2–6–0 No.M3005 departs from Bletchley with a Cambridge train in 1948. These engines were to prove a significant influence in the BR designs of 1951 and later.

The final BR steam design: Riddles 'Class 9F' 2–10–0 No.92012 newly built at Crewe on 30th May 1954 with its immediate LMS predecessor, an unidentified Stanier 'Class 8F' 2–8–0.

former private railways had perfectly adequate machines to carry on had it been so decreed, but Riddles shrewdly involved all the old company design offices in the development of essential elements of the new BR standard practices and gave most of them the overall supervision of at least one of the twelve new designs which he instigated. It fooled nobody at the fundamental level but how could they now complain? Moreover, Riddles was very much a practical man in the Stanier tradition so it was 'all Lombard Street to a China orange' that the fundamental LMS philosophy of ease of maintenance, strict cost-effectiveness and standardisation would prevail over thermodynamic sophistication – and so it turned out to be.

Ultimately, 999 standard engines were built to so-called BR designs but in all honesty, most of them were fundamentally LMS in conception in the Stanier-Ivatt-Riddles tradition (with a few Swindon and Doncaster overtones purely for cosmetic effect!) and arguably only one of them, the Class 9F 2–10–0, really represented anything fundamentally new. It was also, by a long way, the best of the new order; it would have been a 2–8–2 if Riddles had not personally decreed otherwise. Furthermore, whether by accident or design, the last of them all, No. 92220 *Evening Star*, was built not at Crewe but at Swindon and given GWR style cosmetic trimmings by way of compensation! Even so, shades of G.J. Churchward, Swindon-built 9Fs were always more expensive per unit than those from Crewe!

Riddles was not without a sense of humour in spite of all the pressure on him and it was not entirely coincidental that the bulk of the BR steam locomotive fleet was painted black,

BR 'Britannia' 4–6–2 No.70033 *Charles Dickens*, ascends Camden Bank in August 1962 with a down express mostly composed of ex-LNER stock (sic!), in the process passing one of its eventual successors, an unidentified Class 24 diesel-electric on a down empty carriage stock working. It was no coincidence that, being designed by Riddles, the Britannias derived their class name from the old LNWR emblem!

many of them lined out in the traditional LNWR style. Nor was it an accident that the first BR standard 4–6–2 No. 70000 *Britannia* was thus named. It sounded suitably patriotic in 1951 but there was a more subtle meaning – look at the LNWR crest if you doubt it!

So it transpired that the wheel turned full circle, in motive power terms, during the steam history of the L&BR and its successors. It was in at the beginning in the shape of Bury and McConnell and it saw out the final phase with Riddles and the BR standard types. There, it might be supposed, the story would reach a satisfactory conclusion; but the L&BR was not yet finished in terms of its role in British locomotive history and to comprehend its final development, we must, yet again, go back to Sir Josiah Stamp's LMS.

In the early 1930s, the LMS, almost alone of the 'big four' post-1923 railway companies, began seriously to address the mundane but all-important aspect of its infrastructure costs. The end product manifested itself in not a few different ways, not least the rationalisation and improvement of its motive power depot costing, planning and operation, ultimately to become the basis of the post-1947 BR system applied across the whole country. Amongst the various areas put under scrutiny was the cost of shunting goods trains in the various marshalling yards. These were, essentially, the operational preserve of that unsung workhorse of the railway, the shunting tank engine, usually of 0–6–0 configuration; but even these engines spent much of their time doing nothing at all and, in Stamp's analytical mind, this was not 'good news'! Accordingly, he started an effort to make improvements and it first manifested itself in the use of the internal combustion engine.

During the 1930s and 1940s, the LMS conducted wide-ranging and largely successful experiments in the field of diesel shunting locomotives, both diesel-electric and diesel-mechanical. The specific details need not concern us here; they are well recorded in the technical press. What appealed to Stamp was the fact that a diesel shunter could, potentially, be available for 23 hours out of 24 with 'time out' only for re-fuelling plus a further modest amount of time for routine maintenance. Even the most efficient steam locomotive could not match this degree of availability and, in consequence, the LMS never built any new steam shunters after the last of the Fowler Class 3F 0–6–0Ts appeared in 1931. In due course, the

preferred LMS design evolved into the still familiar BR Class 08 0–6–0 diesel electric shunter, the well-nigh ubiquitous inhabitant of almost every BR marshalling yard.

This achievement, in itself, would have been no mean feat but the LMS had loftier ideas. Though Fairburn was, in essence, an electrical engineer and might have been expected to be the leading light in post-Stanier developments of the non-steam kind, he died before his time and it was actually left to Ivatt to supervise the introduction into service of Britain's first main line diesel-electric locomotive in collaboration with the English Electric Company. The first engine appeared just in time to 'beat' the nationalisation deadline, thus becoming the only British main line diesel to carry company markings, a fact which it proudly revealed in December 1947 as LMS No. 10000. A few months later in BR days, it was followed by its twin, the slightly more anonymous No. 10001 and I well remember the mixed feelings which passed through my own mind when I saw the pair of them heading the northbound 'Royal Scot' at Hest Bank in 1949.

They were indeed the harbingers of a new era, but Robert Riddles remained unconvinced and therein lies the root of the

Less well known than the celebrated main-line diesels Nos.10000/10001 were the LMS proposals for an intermediate main line diesel locomotive. The outcome of this thinking did not precede nationalisation but was unveiled at Euston on 14th November 1950 in the shape of No.10800, seen here hauling the 2.05pm press special to Watford on its introduction.

LMS diesel-electric shunting locomotive No.7080, built in 1939 and the forerunner of the modern BR scene.

last part of the story. Riddles has, more than once, been castigated for his apparently stubborn persistence with steam locomotive development when all the smart money was suggesting that diesel traction should be adopted. And at this point, I cannot avoid being slightly personal. Riddles was not opposed to the replacement of steam, whatever people might think. He told me so and he was a totally honest man. Less than 12 months before he died, I had the benefit of conversing with him for almost a whole day and I asked him why he had quit the scene so abruptly in 1953. His reply was revealing and says much in explanation of the somewhat strange events of the 1950s.

In essence, Riddles felt that given the considerable indigenous supplies of coal in Britain, the most logical solution to the traction problem of the railway industry in the 1950s was to go straight from steam to electric as often as possible, using coal to generate the power in both cases – there was, of course, no thought of North Sea oil in those days. He felt that this could best be done by maintaining a fleet of modern, easy to maintain steam locomotives, to 'hold the fort', so to speak, while the main lines were electrified. He even set up an experimental 25 KV evaluation on the Lancaster and Heysham

line in support of his ideas. As far as diesels were concerned, he reckoned that they were mostly justifiable only when the infrastructure costs of total electrification were prohibitive. I well recall the wry smile on his face some thirty years after he left the railway, having resigned on this very issue, when he said: 'And I see nothing that has happened in the last thirty years which makes me want to change my mind.' He also had a few shrewd remarks to make about the stupidity of the loss of freight traffic on the modern railway, but that is outside the immediate discussion!

He, was of course, right. The first generation of BR diesel power in this country, mostly foisted onto the railway by the politicians against the advice of real railwaymen, turned out to be a pretty well unmitigated catalogue of one disaster after another, save for the generally successful diesel multiple unit passenger trains – and these were actually a Riddles idea, instigated before he left! The main line locomotives by contrast, were neither powerful or reliable enough, some were quite unashamedly useless and their subsequent scrapping rate tells all. Even the better examples such as the English Electric Class 40 or the BR Sulzer Class 45/46 engines were no better in terms of absolute haulage power than an LMS

The English-Electric Class 40 was undoubtedly one of the most reliable of the generally rather woeful first generation BR standard diesels and it is perhaps fitting that the 1959 prototype No.D200 has gone to the NRM after 30 years of service. But no-one can objectively claim that the design represented a quantum leap forward in haulage terms from the steam designs it superseded. In this late 1959 view No.D218 is seen ascending Camden Bank with the down 'Shamrock', while a Stanier 2–6–4T deals with empty carriages on the extreme right

'Duchess', LNER A4 or SR 'Merchant Navy' when 'on song'. Furthermore, they had nothing 'in reserve' (unlike a steam or 'straight' electric locomotive) and their comparative capital cost can hardly have brought them into the 'starting frame'! Who could take seriously a locomotive which cost something like four times the cost of the by no means outstanding BR standard 'Britannia' 4–6–2s but which was scarcely capable of pulling a bigger load at any higher speed? It was all very sad and it was only the determined persistence of genuine railwaymen, led by the late and much lamented Gerard Fiennes, which resulted in at least one decent replacement for steam: the celebrated 'Deltics', whose prototype was evaluated on the old LMS main line but whose real fame lay on the East Coast route. But there were simply not enough of them.

Against this background, it is more than somewhat remarkable that the old L&BR, in the event, turned out to be the southern end of the first and for more than 20 years the only 25KV trunk line electrification scheme of the kind envisaged by Riddles as long ago as 1950! That it remained the pioneer for so long after its initiation in 1964 is merely a comment upon the rather strange view we have taken of our railways for most of the period since his time.

In the mid-1960s, the old L&BR became the setting for a new style of 25 KV electrified main line. By 1968, the steam scene had vanished completely and this view at Bletchley was quite typical. It shows Class AL5 electric No. E3080 heading south with the heavy structures of the new overhead catenary very dominant in the view.

A consequence of this new type of pioneering status is that while the L&BR may have been of little relevance in the evaluation of BR diesel traction during the 1950s and subsequently, it has been of more than seminal influence in the development of new forms of main line electric traction. In our present day, of course, we can no longer ascribe locomotive designs to an individual engineer, more's the pity; but we can at least admire the achievements of the Class 87 25KV engines, prosaic though this designation sounds compared with Ramsbottom's 'Ladies of the Lake', Webb's 'Jumbos', Cooke's 'George the Fifths', Fowler's 'Royal Scots', Stanier's 'Duchesses' and Riddles' 'Britannias'. However, the Class 87s are at least in a noble line of pedigree and we can look forward to their successors in the 1990s. Furthermore the welcome reinstatement of the old LNWR's totally random policy of locomotive naming, often in a most inappropriate manner, gives further cause for optimism!

There have, of course, been mistakes and in this context one must mention the abortive Advanced Passenger Train (APT). This was a brave attempt on the part of BR to try and 'fly' with the opposition and would have provided yet another 'marker' in the long line of evolution which has so characterised this celebrated bit of railway. It was a marvellous technical concept but almost inevitably doomed to failure, since there has never been any real sign that our political masters, having taken control of railways in 1948, really understand what public transport is all about. The APT genuinely needed Government support if it was to succeed, but the politicians lacked the sort of backbone which one feels might well have been forthcoming had such people as Lord Stamp or even Richard Moon been in charge.

That Riddles was right in his assessment of the true nature of the modern railway is well exemplified by this 1987 view of a northbound express which, cosmetic considerations apart, is no different in any significant way from its 20 year earlier predecessor at Bletchley: 1966 built Class 86/2 No.86209 *City of Coventry*, based at Willesden no less!

It is also undoubtedly true that the actual electrification of the line out of Euston and its eventual extension to Glasgow along the traditional West Coast route of the old LMS was probably less efficiently carried out than might perhaps have been the case. However, the fact that after a generation of wasted effort, we can now see Riddles' original ideas, first conceived in the context of the L&BR and its successors, being extended into East Anglia and up the East Coast as part of accepted current policy tells all. Thus it is that, 150 years after it was first built, the L&BR and its descendants are still setting the standards which other lines eventually followed. It is no mean achievement.

Chapter 5

TAILPIECE

While dining at Stockton in 1825 with his son Robert and another friend, George Stephenson is alleged to have said to his companions:

"Now lads, I venture to tell you that you will live to see the day when railways will supersede almost all other methods of conveyance in this country – when mail coaches will go by railway and railroads will become the great highway for the King and all his subjects. The time is coming when it will be cheaper for a working man to travel upon a railway than to walk on foot. I know there are great and almost insurmountable difficulties to be encountered; but what I have said will come to pass as sure as you live. I only wish that I may live to see the day, though that I can scarcely hope for, as I know how slow all human progress is . . . "

In fact, of course, he did live to see the day, or at least enough of it to realise that ultimately his prediction would be fulfilled, for the slow progress he mentioned turned out to be a good deal faster than anyone can have either appreciated or even thought possible. Only ten years later, the first trunk lines were being built and, before he died, Stephenson could actually see on the ground all the fundamental elements of the national network. Furthermore, those lines which were open did indeed supersede almost all other forms of travel.

The London and Birmingham was part of this growth and played a crucial part in helping to set the technical and engineering forms which the new mechanised railways were to take. But it did much more than this. As well as initiating a new conception of the very nature of travel, it also played a pivotal role in helping change our whole appreciation of and attitude to the nature of our country itself. One must avoid making spurious or contrived links, but it is astonishingly hard to think of many aspects of modern life which cannot trace at least part of their origins back to ideas pioneered by railways.

The railway was instrumental in establishing whole new meanings for the word 'communication' and such was the ultimate diversification of activity, that its role was to become far more than just a provider of a simple rail journey. Though most of these things were motivated by commercial considerations, in the event, many also turned out to be transformers

of society. Such things as the modern hotel trade, the establishment of the first 'new towns', the development of telecommunications and the standardisation of time immediately come to mind; there are many more. Even the establishment of modern High Street bookselling chains and travel agencies was not without its railway input; the original Mr W.H. Smith actually started his business by selling newspapers at Euston and Mr Thomas Cook started in business by organising railway excursions! Now it would be quite wrong to assign the L&BR and its successors a seminal role in every achievement during the last 150 years but it has played a vital part in more than a significant number.

How, then, does one try to sum up such a story whose outline only has been offered in the preceding pages, with far

more omitted than included? Above all, I suppose, one must still stand a little astonished at the fact that most of the achievements were initiated in a hard-nosed commercial environment with little if any support from the Government, be it Victorian or present century. However, in bringing my thoughts to a conclusion I find that I can only end with what seems in fact to be the ultimate element of irony in the story.

The privately built and operated railways of this country, led by such as the L&BR and its successors, established not only new ways of doing things but a whole new attitude to the concept of public transport as well. One of my favourite quotations is that which is alleged to have been made to new recruits to the management staff of the LNWR when first taking up their appointment: 'Remember you are now a North Western Officer. Take care what you promise but, having promised, take care to fulfil it.' This is no bad advice in the 1980s, but a century or more ago, this philosophy of approach gradually developed not only attitudes of behaviour by railway employees which commended themselves to the public, but also a public expectation of service which still lies latent in our subconscious. We expect the railways to provide a service and are annoyed, disappointed, frustrated or whatever when they do not.

Now it is much to the credit of the private railway industry that, against a commercial background, it could actually help to create this sort of attitude and, indeed, could often deliver a better package in terms of all-round service than can the modern day public controlled and accountable system. But it is false logic to argue from this position, as do some supporters of the modern 'new think', that we can somehow solve the modern transport problem by going back to the old private

system. This could only really work, though I rather doubt it, if those various aspects addressed by the railways in their heyday had remained under unified management and control, but this has not happened. The currently fashionable form of private ownership seems, in the railway context, to consist of little more than fragmentation and asset stripping by transferring assorted bits and pieces of the traditional railway infrastructure back to the private sector, hoping it might work and then standing back in astonishment when it does not. One thing the old private railways did not do was deliberately retreat from the diversification which they had actively promoted.

That they could achieve so much was less a consequence of their private status than the accident which gave them a near monopoly in methodology for almost a century. They were so far ahead of other modes of overland transport that they had no real competition save between themselves. Even that was much diluted by tight Governmental control on fares and freight rates – some would even argue to the detriment of the railways – so the only way one railway could really compete with another was by offering a better service than its rival; the good ones did so by offering the public a better *total* package, including ships, hotels, or anything else that might help and by the end, there was little to choose between any of the bigger companies. At the most fundamental level, the territorial 'grouping' of 1923, while maybe offering some operational economies, did not really solve anything and neither for that matter did nationalisation.

The real competition was that which came about as a result of alternative *forms* of transport: cars, buses, aircraft &c.; and I have tried to indicate how the development of these later modes drew much on the ideas created by the railway. Whatever their faults, the old railway companies knew, understood and developed the totality of transport; their rival modes saw this, realised that it made sense and responded in kind. It is, to quote but one example, inconceivable that one should go on holiday by air these days without there being a close tie-in between the airline and the hotel at destination.

Since railway nationalisation, the same kind of misunderstanding about the nature of transport which has always bedevilled Parliament since Victoria's time has continued to characterise most of our politicians, whatever their party colour; however, because of public ownership they have felt free to interfere in the day-to-day management of the industry in a way that would never have been allowed to the shareholders of the old companies. One prime minister, who shall remain nameless, was even unable to appreciate that 'trains' and 'locomotives' were two different things! This fundamental confusion has then been further overlain with the 'nationalised versus private', 'road versus rail' and many other politically inspired nostra to the eventual benefit of no-one save those with their own vested interests to promote. It is interesting in this context to reflect on the fact that the railways have, in the intermittent periods of avoidance of political interference during the last forty years, usually done best when run by people who actually understand the 'nature of the beast'. This is not, of course, to say that there should have been no line closures or rationalisation, nor am I arguing that the railways should not be under public ownership. It is merely a plea for Government to create an environment in which the railways can be operated by people who fully understand the nature of the industry they serve and then let them get on with it, free from interference.

In so far as current political thinking is allowing railway management to move away from what has often seemed, since 1948, to be a quasi-social service obligation to do little more than keep many underemployed railwaymen at work, regardless of need or operational efficiency – the old companies would no more have done that than do the railway's modern rivals(!) – then I am all for it. But to the extent that the railways still have to suffer political interference in their operation by people with no real knowledge, then I have grave doubts as to whether the politicians have yet got it right. There are, fortunately, a few encouraging signs that the modern railway is now, at least, being allowed some of the operational freedoms of the kind more familiar in the old company days and it is to be hoped that this is not a false dawn. If it is not, then future omens, though still rather faint, are perhaps not entirely unhopeful. However, I cannot believe it was right for the railways to have so many bits of their own 'total package' hived off elsewhere (road haulage, ships, hotels &c) that they are now unable to give the fully integrated service they once could offer.

We have maybe got a little far from the London and Birmingham Railway in the last few paragraphs, but if there is a message at all in the tale of this line, it is that its historical significance stems from the fact that it was conceived, built and operated for more than a century by confident men, free from too much ignorant interference, who firstly could see its purpose and relevance to their own time and secondly, could fully understand its nature and make it work. In this respect, it set the pattern for much which followed and for it to continue to have significance, this message must still hold true.

Just about a century separates these two fine paintings of Euston, both held in the National Railway Museum.
The upper view shows the original arrangement of Philip Hardwick's noble Propyleum and flanking pavilions.
The lower picture is a design study for the impressive Art Deco structure which the LMS proposed but never built.